MW00626663

GRAVE INTENTIONS:

A Comprehensive Guide to Preserving Historic Cemeteries in Georgia

Christine Van Voorhies

Georgia Department
of Natural Resources

Historic Chattahoochee
Commission

www.gashpo.org   hcc@alalinc.net

This book was published by the Historic Preservation Division of the Georgia Department of Natural Resources in cooperation with the Historic Chattahoochee Commission

Publication of this work was generously funded by the
Historic Chattahoochee Commission

P. O. Box 942	*P. O. Box 33*
LaGrange, GA 30241	*Eufaula, AL 36072-0033*

706-845-8440
hcc@alalinc.net

Library of Congress Cataloging-in-Publication Data

Van Voorhies, Christine, 1948-
   Grave intentions : a comprehensive guide to preserving historic cemeteries in Georgia/
Christine Van Voorhies.--1st ed.
      p. cm.
   Includes bibliographical references (p.).
   ISBN 0-945477-15-5 (paperback)
      1. Cemeteries--Conservation and restoration--Georgia--Handbooks, manuals, etc. 2.
   Historic sites--Conservation and restoration--Georgia--Handbooks, manuals, etc. 3.
   Historic preservation--Georgia--Handbooks, manuals, etc. 4.
   Georgia--Antiquities--Collection and preservation--Handbooks, manuals, etc. I. Title.

   F287.V36 2003
   363.6'9--dc21   2003047876

ISBN 0-945477-15-5

Creative direction:
   Wynocker-Beckwith Ltd.
Cover design & typography:
   Jason Echols
Photos:
   Georgia Department of Natural Resources,
   Historic Preservation Division and Wildlife Resources Division

GRAVE INTENTIONS:

A Comprehensive Guide to
Preserving Historic Cemeteries in Georgia

Christine Van Voorhies

Secretary of State
214 State Capitol
Atlanta, Georgia 30334

Cathy Cox
SECRETARY OF STATE
(404) 656-2881

    We have all seen cemeteries as we drive through Georgia's towns and countryside. Whether they are small family plots in a pasture or large graveyards in one of our cities, cemeteries are tangible, and often beautiful, links to our ancestors. Despite their importance, however, cemeteries are frequently threatened in our fast-paced world. In Georgia, the Historic Preservation Division of the Department of Natural Resources and the Secretary of State's Office work together to safeguard historic as well as modern cemeteries and insure that all human graves are given respect.

    Grave Intentions is a book designed to answer questions and give guidance about protecting cemeteries. The Georgia Secretary of State avidly supports this publication, recognizing it will meet a wide-ranging need for assistance of this type in Georgia. We are happy to see the culmination of this effort by the Historic Preservation Division of DNR and the Historic Chattahoochee Commission, which will be of significant benefit to people across our great state as well as the entire southeastern region.

Sincerely,

Cathy Cox

The Honorable Sonny Perdue
Governor, State of Georgia

Mr. Lonice C. Barrett, Commissioner
Georgia Department of Natural Resources

Dr. W. Ray Luce, Director
Historic Preservation Division of Georgia
Department of Natural Resources

ACKNOWLEDGEMENTS

The Georgia Department of Natural Resources (DNR) Historic Preservation Division (HPD) exists to promote the respect, preservation, and use of historic places for a better Georgia. As our state grows, long forgotten cemeteries are rediscovered, often in the course of construction or other ground-disturbing activity. As a result, more and more people are contacting HPD for advice on protecting and maintaining historic cemeteries.

This book is an attempt to offer guidance on these historic cemetery issues in an easy-to-use format. It is based on an earlier manuscript by Kenneth H. Thomas, Jr., HPD historian. I owe a great deal to Mr. Thomas for his earlier work as well as his encouragement and collaboration on this book. I also thank Ray Luce, HPD Division Director, for his support and commitment to bringing this book to publication. The printing of this book was made possible by the generous financial support of the Historic Chattahoochee Commission, an agency of the states of Alabama and Georgia involved in the promotion of tourism and historic preservation throughout the lower Chattahoochee Valley. Sincere thanks go to HCC Executive Director Douglas Purcell and the board of directors for their unhesitating positive response to the manuscript. The Historic Chattahoochee Commission and the Historic Preservation Division will direct proceeds from this book back into future cemetery and preservation projects for the continued benefit of the public.

I gratefully acknowledge the review of the book and comments by Ted Brooke, Kenneth Gibbs, Gretchen Brock, Paul McLarty, Carole Moore, John R. (Chip) Morgan, John Sheftall, Helen Talley-McRae, Kenneth H. Thomas, Jr., James Van Voorhies, and John Walden. I thank Dan Parrish and Jim Lockhart for their assistance in procuring many of the wonderful images that enhance this book. In particular, I'd like to thank David C. Crass, state archaeologist and HPD Archaeological Services Unit manager, for his encouragement and unfailing support in all aspects of this publication from conception through printing.

Christine Van Voorhies

TABLE OF CONTENTS

GRAVE INTENTIONS

INTRODUCTION

Georgians are becoming aware that we may lose the unique heritage our historic and prehistoric cemeteries contain as our economy booms and development expands in all parts of the state. Individuals and various groups across the state have begun voicing their concern about protecting this heritage. Involved citizens are raising questions about how to restore, protect, and preserve cemeteries; those questions are frequently directed to the Historic Preservation Division (HPD) of the Georgia Department of Natural Resources (DNR).

The legal responsibility for private or abandoned cemeteries lies with the owners of the property where the graves are located. Therefore, our state agency does not have law enforcement authority and cannot regulate preservation on private property. However, we do place priority on protecting our heritage and believe much can be done by working within the existing laws, drawing on community support and values. We share the significant concern of many Georgians about threats to historic and prehistoric cemeteries. All human burials, whether they are thousands of years old or much more recent, should be accorded respect even as we carefully study cemeteries to plan their restoration, to insure their future protection, and to document the history they can tell us. The Georgia Council on American Indian Concerns, while speaking primarily about American Indian resources, captures this sentiment quite well.

INTRODUCTION

Three fundamental principles guide all state and federal laws dealing with human remains, artifacts, [and] archeological sites . . . The first is respect for religious beliefs of all Americans, including American Indians. The second is respect for the dead. The third is the protection of archeological sites for the benefit of all Americans, not just a few, because these sites are part of our common heritage.[1]

To that end, it is our goal to support protection efforts by providing helpful information for use by anyone undertaking a cemetery preservation project. This guide to resources and technical assistance has been designed to be a starting point for individuals or groups, as it:

◆ addresses issues to be considered, ranging from determining who owns a cemetery, contacting descendants, recording and marking a cemetery, to restoration plans and protection from vandals and development threats.

◆ suggests ways to solve some common problems by citing previous projects completed in Georgia, listing publications on specific topics, and recommending various ways to approach particular questions.

◆ lists who to consult with or contact on particular aspects of cemetery preservation, publications by experts in the field of cemetery restoration, and other sources for information.

Modern development often threatens rural cemeteries.

[1] Council on American Indian Concerns, *Artifact Collecting and the Law in Georgia: What's Legal and What's Not*, available from Council on American Indian Concerns, 2 Martin Luther King Jr. Drive, Suite 1352, East Tower, Atlanta, GA 30334; http://www.ganet.org/indcouncil

DEFINITION OF A CEMETERY

Georgia law defines a cemetery as "any land . . . dedicated to and used, or intended to be used, for interment of human remains."[2] Georgia law also states "the fact that the area was used for burial purposes shall be evidence that it was set aside for burial purposes."[3]

A burial place for one or more individuals can range from prehistoric American Indian burials to those in a modern perpetual care cemetery. The following types of burial grounds or cemeteries are within the scope of the law: family, church, community, public (such as a city cemetery), corporate (privately owned and maintained cemeteries, usually perpetual care), military, institutional (such as at the state prison or state hospital), prehistoric burials, and isolated burials (such as someone buried by the side of the road on a migration route or during wartime).

In this document, we address historic and prehistoric burials. "Historic" is a term used to describe a cemetery that is older than 50 years, but was established after documented European contact occurred in Georgia around A.D. 1540. Burials that existed before A.D. 1540 are described as "prehistoric." For the sake of brevity, we have used the word "cemetery" to mean prehistoric as well as historic burial places.

*Active,
historic cemetery,
Oakland Cemetery,
Atlanta, GA.*

---

[2] Official Code of Georgia (Ga. Code) § 36-72-2[5] (2001).
[3] Ga. Code § 36-72-2[3] (2001).

1839

Sep. 9th I performed the rite of burial over the body of
Daniel aged about 6 years.   P. Whelan

Oct. 16th   body o
Nathan ag   an

January 2   the bod
of Mary A   s
                                                     an

April 20t   e body
John Fynn   Galway,
Ireland   an

August 22   ver the
body of E   of
Ireland,   an

Fencing can help protect abandoned cemeteries.

April 16th - Died during my absence Mary Murphy aged 10
years   Peter Whalen

Sep 20th I performed the rite of burial over the body of
Mary Ann   alen

Oct --th   body of
Richard M   Longfo
Ireland,   gton Wi
Co.   lan
- - - - -
Page 88

I perform   na Quig
aged abou   an

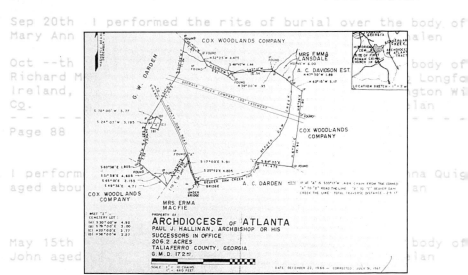
A typical land plat on which a cemetery is marked.

October 25th   over the boo
of Patrick Norton, a native of the Co Tipprery, Ireland,
aged about fifty years.   Peter Whelan

1844

March   I performed   rial over the body of
Samuel aged about sixty years   Peter Whelan

4

CEMETERY OWNERSHIP, ACCESS, ABANDONED CEMETERIES

OWNERSHIP

 One of the most important questions to be considered before attempting any cemetery restoration or protection effort is "who owns the cemetery land?" The landowner's permission should be obtained before going onto the property. Even when a cemetery appears abandoned and in ruins, it is still on property owned by someone. In the past, when land was sold, the deeds often included an express reservation of land for burial purposes, stating that a family's farm or plantation property was being sold "except one acre reserved for the family graveyard" or where persons were already buried. Notations on plats may also have indicated the existence of Indian or slave burials. Later deeds and plats may have inadvertently omitted this information. However, once such an express reservation has been given, it is thereafter considered to be valid and in effect regardless of whether or not the current property deed specifically mentions the cemetery. The landowner on whose property the cemetery is located can still have fee simple title to the whole tract of land, but that title includes the reservation for the cemetery.

It may be necessary to search the county land deeds or tax records to determine who currently owns the property. Property deeds are filed in the office of the clerk of the superior court of the county in which the property is located. Tax records, including maps, will be found in the tax commissioner's office. These records are open for public use. Contact the clerk of the superior court and the tax commissioner's office in your county courthouse for further information about using these records. If a current owner cannot be easily ascertained from the deed or tax records, then further research may be necessary, such as inquiring of local funeral directors about family members of anyone recently buried in the cemetery or about their knowledge of other claimants to the cemetery plots.

ACCESS

Currently no law specifically addresses access to cemeteries. However, existing real property laws have been interpreted, as a result of cases brought to court, to mean that the heirs of those buried in the cemetery have an easement over the property that adjoins the cemetery. Pindar's Georgia Real Estate Law and Procedure with Forms by Daniel F. Hinkel presents this interpretation, stating that the easement gives heirs the right to prevent trespass that disturbs the burials, the right to consent to or prevent disinterment, and the right of ingress and egress for attending the burials.[4] It should be noted that in some cases heirs might consider the well-intentioned cleanup efforts of non-family, concerned citizens to be a disturbance rather than assistance.

While Georgia law at present is unclear on these issues, standard legal practice acknowledges access and maintenance rights as described in Hinkel's publication referenced above. It is also generally accepted that those desiring access will negotiate a reasonable agreement with the landowner. Therefore, we advise even heirs who have implied easement rights to seek landowner permission for access, including negotiating an agreement with the landowner regarding notification of intent to visit, the method and frequency of visitation, and passageway to be used.

---

[4] Daniel F. Hinkel, "§ 8-44.1 Burial and cemetery easements," in *Pindar's Georgia Real Estate Law and Procedure With Forms*, Fifth Edition, Volume 1 (Norcross, GA: The Harrison Company, 1998), 469.

If you are interested in verifying the location of a prehistoric grave, cleaning up a badly overgrown cemetery, or in locating a family burial plot, we recommend that you do not cross another's property without prior permission to do so. If there is no public road into the cemetery, then determine the identity of the surrounding landowners and ask permission to cross their property.

Proving existence of unmarked cemeteries

It may be necessary to prove that graves exist before the landowner will allow access to his property to look for the cemetery, if it is unknown to him. Many graves are not marked at all. This may be the result of religious beliefs or cultural tradition, or the lack of means to do so. Graves might be unknown because the marker material, such as fieldstone or wood, has long since eroded or deteriorated. Also, grave markers may be hidden by vegetation, moved, or stolen. Proof of the existence of Indian burials or a family, community, or church cemetery thus lies in archaeological information, historical and genealogical information, deeds, county tax records or tax maps, the word of a local mortician if a burial has occurred there in the last few decades, or oral tradition.

Historic maps are a good source to consult because occasionally information has been changed or left off the newer, updated versions. The Georgia Department of Archives and History has a large collection of historic maps available for use in research. Another good map research source is the map room of the Science Library at the University of Georgia in Athens. There you'll find aerial maps produced by the U.S. Department of Agriculture Soil Conservation Service (now known as the Natural Resources Conservation Service) that might show features indicating cemeteries not marked on other maps. You may want to also see what records are held by the local historical society, any city or county preservation planning staff, and the preservation planner at your regional development center (RDC). Ask if they are aware of any cemeteries in the location you are researching. If you need information about which RDC region your county is in, you may contact the Community Planning Coordinator in the Historic Preservation Division office, phone 404.656.2840; or you may view a map and access links to all the RDCs at the Carl Vinson Institute of Government Web site: http://www.cviog.uga.edu/Projects/gainfo/regionmaps/rdc.htm.

Remember, even when you are not sure whether the cemetery exists, permission should be obtained from the property owner to go onto the property for the purpose of trying to locate the cemetery.

Consulting heirs

If you believe you have family members buried in a particular cemetery, documentation to that effect will be useful in establishing your right to access the cemetery. This documentation can take the form of copies of property deeds, obituaries of people buried there, church records, or some statement of your genealogical research showing a family connection. If available, the county probate records may also be helpful.

If you don't have ancestors in the cemetery but are interested in its restoration or protection for other reasons, then the heirs of people buried there must be consulted and their permission granted before any activity on the property is undertaken. To locate heirs, you might start with the name of one deceased person and use genealogical resources to find other members of the family and/or descendants. Other things to do: research church records, do a query over the Internet at genealogical sites such as http://www.usgenweb.org, contact any local genealogical or historical society, put a paid advertisement for heirs in the legal organ of the county or in smaller communities, write a letter to the editor of the local newspaper requesting information, or hire a professional genealogist to track the descendants for you. The Georgia Genealogical Society maintains a list of researchers for hire. You can contact them at their Web site: www.gagensociety.org/members.htm or by regular mail at P.O. Box 54575, Atlanta, GA 30308-0575.

Church cemeteries

A cemetery that was originally associated with a church might appear to be abandoned because the church building and congregation are gone. It is possible that the land on which the church rested was either sold to another owner or transferred to the church where the surviving members transferred their membership. If the congregation died out without any transfer of memberships or land, then the heirs of the last members would hold the easement rights discussed above. Inquiring of the local funeral directors about any recent burials in the cemetery and a search of the county deed records may be the best ways to ascertain with whom the title to the property now rests. Then the proper landowner(s) may be consulted about restoration or protection of the cemetery.

Mt. Gilead Baptist Church, Lumpkin County, GA.

City cemeteries

Oakland Cemetery, Atlanta, GA.

A city cemetery is the responsibility of the city government unless jurisdiction has been assigned to a different agency, historical society, or other nonprofit organization. It is also imperative to ask permission of the heirs to repair or clean up a family's lot in a publicly owned cemetery, such as a city cemetery. Although seeking the heirs is important, it is not necessary that all living descendants be located. Often all that is needed is proof that a reasonable search was made. For that proof, use documentation gathered when doing research using the methods described in the section titled **Consulting heirs,** page 8.

ABANDONED CEMETERIES LAW

Marked graves in abandoned cemeteries can become obscured by vegetation.

Georgia's Abandoned Cemeteries and Burial Grounds law, listed in the Official Code of Georgia (Ga. Code), addresses ownership and responsibility for upkeep of abandoned cemeteries. It provides a definition of what an abandoned cemetery is under the law and then how a county or municipality is authorized but not required to preserve it:

Ga. Code § 36-72-2. *Definitions. As used in this chapter, the term:* (1) "Abandoned cemetery" means a cemetery which shows signs of neglect including, without limitation, the unchecked growth of vegetation, repeated and unchecked acts of vandalism, or the disintegration of grave markers or boundaries and for which no person can be found who is legally responsible and financially capable of the upkeep of such cemetery.

Ga. Code § 36-72-3. *Authority of counties and municipalities to preserve abandoned cemeteries.*
Counties . . . and municipalities . . . are authorized, jointly and severally, to preserve and protect any abandoned cemetery or any burial ground which the county or municipality determines has been abandoned or is not being maintained by the person who is legally responsible for its upkeep . . . to expend public money in connection therewith . . . and to exercise the power of eminent domain to acquire any interest in land necessary for that purpose.

If a cemetery you are concerned about can be defined as abandoned under the law, then you may consider approaching the local governing authority to request that the municipality or county take on the responsibility of maintaining and protecting the cemetery, as authorized by this law. It may help to have a copy of the law in hand or the Official Code of Georgia citation for reference when discussing this, as government officials may not be familiar with these infrequently used statutes relating to cemeteries (see Appendix B for the text of this statute).

If the gravesite you are concerned about is suspected to be a prehistoric burial, then contact the Council on American Indian Concerns, which was created by the Georgia legislature under Ga. Code § 44-12-280 *et seq.* to help protect Indian graves and burial objects. Indian burials are covered under laws protecting human remains and archaeological sites – Ga. Code § 31-21-6, § 31-21-44, §12-3-621 (see Appendix B for the text of these laws). This council has the authority to make recommendations regarding suspected or identified Indian burials. They have the resources to assist in getting an evaluation of the gravesite, verifying it as Indian, identifying descendants or culturally affiliated groups that might be associated with the remains, and directing protection plans. The council can be contacted at 2 Martin Luther King Jr. Drive, Suite 1352, East Tower, Atlanta, GA 30334, phone 404.656.2770; http://www.ganet.org/ indcouncil.

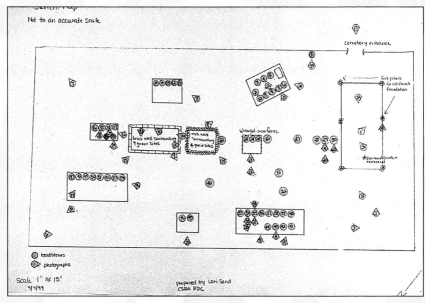

Sample sketch map of cemetery features.

2

RECORDING, COMMEMORATING A CEMETERY

RECORDING

Historic cemetery recordation projects are often undertaken by genealogical or historical societies but can be done by individuals as well. There are many good examples of published completed projects at the Georgia Department of Archives and History, 330 Capitol Avenue, Atlanta, GA 30334, and other libraries. Another excellent source is the <u>Georgia Cemetery Directory and Bibliography of Georgia Cemetery Reference Sources</u>, a guide to previously published cemetery records, written and published by Ted O. Brooke in 1985. There are also good examples on the Internet of recorded cemeteries, along with information on how to properly record a cemetery (for Web sites, see Appendix A).

Recording a cemetery can mean several different things. You may want to merely see that the geographical location of a cemetery is marked on maps and recorded in the proper public records. On a finer scale, you may want to record the layout of the cemetery landscape, noting the number of graves and how they are aligned, what other features are in the graveyard, and where the boundaries are. An even more specific recordation project would be that of writing down all readable legends and genealogical information on the tombstones, as well as noting decorative motifs employed. It is strongly recommended that, along with written records, some type of visual record be made, either with photographs or a video recording. The scale of your project will, of course, depend on what is deemed necessary and what can be executed with the money and labor available. For your use, a sample general recording form is included at the end of this booklet, along with a sample map illustrating one way to record the layout of graves and landscape features.

The following steps are general in nature to guide the planning of your project.

Step 1. Document the accurate location of the cemetery. If possible, calculate the Universal Transverse Mercator (UTM) coordinates or the latitude and longitude coordinates, using a Global Positioning System (GPS) unit. Small hand-held GPS units are readily available at discount retail stores for a reasonable price and can be used even by a novice. Many GPS units can be programmed to determine either the UTMs or latitude and longitude. If you do not know how to calculate these coordinates or do not have the necessary equipment to do so, then note the county, the nearest town, and then the cemetery's relative position to that town, using the cardinal directions. A Georgia highway or county map and a compass will be useful for these determinations.

In some instances, you may be attempting to locate a cemetery known to you only through secondhand information. This could be difficult because information on its location may vary, coming from sources such as hearsay, older community members, or old maps. Even a visit to the suspected site of the cemetery may not be definitive if the graves are no longer marked and the area is overgrown. In those instances, it will be necessary to hire an archaeologist, professional land surveyor, historian, or other expert to help determine whether you have indeed found a cemetery and the location of its boundaries. For guidance in selecting a professional archaeologist or historian, contact the Historic Preservation Division for the list of archaeological consulting firms in Georgia and a copy of the *Professional Qualifications Standards: History, Archaeology, Architectural History, and Historic Architecture.* To find a professional land surveyor in your area, you might consult The Surveying and Mapping Society of Georgia (SAMSOG), P. O. Box 778, Douglasville, GA 30133-1272, phone 770.489.1440. You can easily do a search at their Web site, www.samsog.org. Click on Member Services and in the drop-down menu, select Member Search. The screen that comes up will allow you to enter your town or county name, and it will bring up the SAMSOG members in that location.

Step 2. **Determine the boundaries:** You cannot assume that the currently cleared or marked (fenced, walled, planted, or landscaped) area corresponds to the actual boundary that includes all the graves. Often burials are located outside of the area presently marked as the cemetery. This happens when some graves have lost their markers and therefore are not easily seen when a fence is put in. Not all graves would have been marked with permanent stone markers. Wood and simple stones both have historically been used as common grave-marker materials. These are highly subject to rot and displacement, obscuring the location of graves they marked. Therefore, the actual burial ground could extend over a much larger area than is easily discernible to the untrained eye. While the ground surface can be examined for grave-sized depressions, a professional archaeologist or other expert may need to be called in to accurately determine the location of all unmarked graves.

A good example of the research involved in establishing the dimensions of a cemetery and the actual existence of unmarked graves can be found in the article by Roy S. Dickens, Jr. and Robert L. Blakely, "Preliminary Report on Archaeological Investigations in Oakland Cemetery, Atlanta, Georgia," <u>The Conference on Historic Site Archaeology Papers</u>, XIII (1978) 286-314. A copy of this document is on file at the Atlanta History Center, 130 West Paces Ferry Road, NW, Atlanta, GA 30305-1366; main number 404.814.4000; research room 404.814.4040; http://www.atlantahistorycenter.com.

Step 3. Record the exact location of the cemetery on a map.

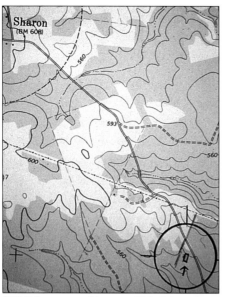

While there are several good base maps you could use, the most accurate and permanent is the U.S. Geologic Survey (U.S.G.S.) topographic map series. These can be purchased for a small fee from the Georgia Geologic Survey's map room, 19 Martin Luther King, Jr. Drive, Atlanta, GA 30334; phone 404.656.3214. Information about reading and using these maps, as well as ordering information, is on the U.S.G.S. Web site: http:// mcmcweb.er.usgs.gov/ topomaps. The maps are marked with the UTM grid lines and numbers so the coordinates for a spot on the map can be determined. Topographic maps might also be available at map stores or outdoor recreation equipment stores, and some of Georgia's regional development centers have these maps available for purchase at a nominal fee.

U.S.G.S. topographic map, N.E. GA, scale 1:24,000.

Another good choice is a map that shows the land lot and district divisions, such as a county tax map. Check with the tax commissioner's office at the county courthouse to obtain copies of tax maps.

A Georgia highway map may be the most easily obtained and certainly can be used. You might want to reduce it to just the pertinent quadrant of the state, but be sure to keep the portion of the map you section out large enough to show the county and nearest towns.

Step 4. **Record observable information about the graves them-selves and the tombstone inscriptions.** There are several excellent sources to guide you in the proper way to record these data. Some books and Web sites listed in Appendix A can offer assistance with cemetery recording methods. See more information under **RESTORING A CEMETERY,** page 25. The following books are highly recommended:

Ted O. Brooke, ed., <u>The Cemetery Book: Cemetery Preservation, Restoration, and Recording</u> (Atlanta: Georgia Genealogical Society, 1989). This book is out of print and is currently being revised. Check with the Georgia Genealogical Society for availability at http://www.GaGenSociety.org, or P.O. Box 54575, Atlanta, GA 30308-0575, or e-mail at ggs@gagensociety.org. The book may also be available at local libraries or larger genealogical libraries. For fur-ther advice regarding recording cemeteries, Mr. Brooke may be con-tacted at 2055 Foster Drive, Cumming, GA 30040.

Lynette Strangstad, <u>A Graveyard Preservation Primer</u> (Walnut Creek, California: AltaMira Press, 1995; originally published by the American Association for State and Local History, 1988). Ms. Strangstad is a nationally recognized expert in this field.

Sharyn Thompson, <u>Florida's Historic Cemeteries: A Preservation Handbook</u> (Columbia, SC: Historic Tallahassee Preservation Board, 1989). This is another excellent guide.

Photography is an excellent method of recording cemetery and grave marker information. See Mary-Ellen Jones' book <u>Photographing Tombstones: Equipment and Techniques</u>, American Association for State and Local History Technical Leaflet #92, pub-lished by the American Association for State and Local History in 1977.

Step 5. **Have the cemetery recorded in public records** once you have noted the cemetery on a U.S.G.S. topographic map or other appropriate base map. There are several reasons for this. First, you can help other interested researchers use the data you have gathered. Second, by recording the cemetery in public records, such as tax maps, deed records, plats, and Department of Transportation maps, you establish public knowledge of that cemetery for legal purposes, thereby bringing it under the protection of Georgia law.

The Abandoned Cemeteries and Burial Grounds law states "No **known** cemetery, burial ground, human remains, or burial object shall be knowingly disturbed by the owner or occupier of the land . . . for the purposes of developing or changing the use of any part of such land unless a permit is first obtained."[5] Therefore, the courts may only hear complaints about a cemetery being threatened by development or other disturbance if there has been some public knowledge about the existence of the cemetery. If, for example, a developer was unaware a cemetery existed on his property, it will be difficult under this law to hold him responsible for disturbing it.

Ensure that unknown or obscured graveyards are marked in public records.

[5] Ga. Code § 36-72-1(2001).

To have the cemetery marked on public records:

♦ On county tax maps, contact the tax commissioner's office at the county courthouse. Ted Brooke, in his book <u>The Cemetery Book: Cemetery Preservation, Restoration & Recording</u>, suggests that "county tax offices will usually not put cemeteries on their maps unless they are found within deed records and are plotted by a surveyor, showing exact dimensions. If they resist, show them copies of the various Georgia laws requiring protection of cemeteries and ask them to reconsider their position."[6]

♦ Adding a cemetery notation to the land deed may require the services of an attorney to file an affidavit of title and have it cross-referenced to the property owner's deed. If you own the property containing a cemetery that has not previously been marked on the deed, then you may want to just keep the documentation about the cemetery with your copy of the deed and other property-related records for safe keeping. Then whenever the property is sold in the future, that information can be incorporated into the new deed by the attorney handling the land transfer.

♦ To add the cemetery to the appropriate Georgia highway map, send the documentation to the Georgia Department of Transportation, 5025 New Peachtree Road, Chamblee, GA 30341; phone 770.986.1366.

♦ The U.S. Forest Service publishes maps of its forests and will add cemetery information to these maps. Contact the U.S. Forest Service, 1755 Cleveland Highway, Gainesville, GA 30501; phone 770.536.0541.

♦ The cemetery information can also be submitted to the county historical organization, local genealogical organization, and to the local or nearest public library. Send each institution a copy of your findings with a map and photographs.

[6] Ted O. Brooke, *The Cemetery Book: Cemetery Preservation, Restoration & Recording* (Atlanta: The Georgia Genealogical Society, 1989), 39.

♦ Donate a copy of the record you have made to the Georgia Department of Archives and History, 330 Capitol Avenue, Atlanta, GA 30334 for their permanent file.

♦ See that the information is recorded in the state cemetery database, which is known as the Georgia Cemetery Mapping Project and is housed at the Georgia Archaeological Site File, University of Georgia, 110 Riverbend Road, Athens, GA 30602-4702. Contact them by phone at 706.542.8737 or go to their Web site http://shapiro.anthro.uga.edu/GASF for assistance regarding contributing cemetery information.

If you are interested in compiling a book of all the cemeteries in your county, some good examples from Georgia counties are available, and there may be grant money available to publish such a book. There are a number of cemetery books at the Georgia Department of Archives and History, 330 Capitol Avenue, Atlanta, GA 30334, phone 404.656.2393. Before making a trip to their location, you may want to look online at their collections. Go to their Web site (a part of the Secretary of State's Web site) at http://www.sos.state.ga.us, and click on "Archives" home page, select "search," then "catalog," and click on "Georgia Archives GIL." That will bring up a page where you can launch a search for the keyword "cemetery." A good example is <u>Cemeteries of Oglethorpe County, Georgia</u> published by Historic Oglethorpe County, Inc. in 1995, which is available at the Department of Archives and History. Another quick reference on how a cemetery book should be written is "Guidelines for Cemetery Books," prepared by Ted O. Brooke, 1998, online at www.GaGenSociety.org/ggscem.htm.

Money may be available for publishing a cemetery record book through grants from the R. J. Taylor, Jr. Foundation, which is interested in providing for the publication of appropriately retrieved genealogical information from public and private records. The foundation can be contacted at SunTrust Bank - Atlanta, R. J. Taylor, Jr. Foundation, P.O. Box 4655, MC 221, Atlanta, GA 30302. Information

is available at their Web site: http://www.taylorfoundation.org. Their Web site also has some short, clear guidelines on what information a cemetery book should contain. A number of the cemetery books located at the Department of Archives and History were published with funding from the Taylor Foundation.

COMMEMORATING

Signs show a cemetery is being monitored.

Interested citizens often want to bring attention to a previously unmarked cemetery to help insure its protection and/or commemorate the dead buried there. Signs can demonstrate that the cemetery is being monitored and could list whom to contact for access. The danger in marking a previously obscure cemetery is that it may lure vandals to the site. Please consider vulnerability to acts of vandalism before you make plans to post signage of any type. See more discussion of this issue under **PROTECTING A CEMETERY, Looting and Vandalism,** page 46.

Georgia historical markers

The Georgia Historical Marker program was begun in 1951 and administered until recently by the Department of Natural Resources. The current program is managed by the Georgia Historical Society. Due to the limited number of new markers funded each year and the statewide nature of the program, it is unlikely that a marker will be authorized for a family or church cemetery. For more information about the program or how to apply, contact the Georgia Historical Society, 501 Whitaker Street, Savannah, GA 31499, phone 912.651.2125; http://www.georgiahistory.com; e-mail for library and archives: ghslib@georigahistory.com; administrative e-mail: ghs@georgiahistory.com.

National Register of Historic Places

The National Register of Historic Places (NR), created in 1966, is a federal program of the National Park Service, Department of the Interior, which is administered in Georgia by the Historic Preservation Division. This program recognizes the significance of our historic heritage and the need to preserve it, but it confers no absolute power to protect or rescue

Plaques are not provided by the National Register program.

any property from imminent destruction or damage. Whether or not the property is listed in the National Register, a landowner has the right to do whatever he/she chooses to the property, including demolition, unless local zoning forbids such action or unless human remains would be disturbed. Further, property cannot be listed in the National Register without the landowner's permission. This program **does not** provide a plaque to mark a National Register listing.

The National Register ordinarily prohibits the listing of cemeteries, including graves of historical figures, unless they are "integral parts of [historic] districts that do meet the [National Register] criteria or if they fall within the following categories: . . . a religious property [that] derives its primary significance from architectural or artistic distinction or historical importance; a grave of a historical figure . . . of outstanding importance and if there is no other appropriate site or building directly associated with his or her productive life; or a cemetery [that] derives its primary significance from graves of persons of transcendent importance, from age, from distinctive design features, or from association with historic events."[7] Therefore, small family cemeteries and church cemeteries without a surviving church building are unlikely to qualify for listing on the NR.

---

[7] Elisabeth Walton Potter and Beth M. Boland, *Guidelines for Evaluating and Registering Cemeteries and Burial Places*, National Register Bulletin, No. 41 (Washington: U.S. Department of the Interior, National Park Service, 1992), 15-16.

Examples of Georgia cemeteries which have met the exception to this rule and have been listed in the NR include several of the large, landscaped, city cemeteries such as Oakland (Atlanta), Laurel Grove (Savannah) and Rose Hill (Macon); those within a historic district, where most of a town is being nominated (Madison); and those associated with historic farm or plantation housing (John Frank Mathews Plantation and Cemetery, Talbot County).

Other cemeteries listed in the NR have been those where a historic church building survives with its adjoining historic cemetery, such as the Green Grove Church, Cemetery, and School (Lumpkin); B'nai Israel Synagogue and Cemetery (Thomasville); and Omer Christian Church and Cemetery (Barrow County).

Another exception to this rule would be prehistoric burial sites that may be eligible for the NR if they have yielded, or may be likely to yield, information important in pre-history or history. Under Criterion D of the

B'nai Israel Synagogue, Thomasville, GA.

NR, these sites have to meet two requirements: first, the property must contribute to our understanding of human history or prehistory; and second, the information must be considered important. This criterion for listing in the NR is most often applied to archaeological sites, although it can also apply to buildings, structures, and objects that contain important information.[8]

For more information about the NR program, contact the Survey and National Register Unit of the Historic Preservation Division. There is also information available on the division's Web site at http://www.gashpo.org and at the National Park Service Web site, http://www.cr.nps.gov/nr.

---

[8] Rebecca H. Shrimpton, editor, *How to Apply the National Register Criteria for Evaluation*, National Register Bulletin (Washington: U.S. Department of the Interior, National Park Service, 1997), 21.

Bonaventure Cemetery, Savannah, GA.

RESTORING A CEMETERY

RESTORATION PLAN – GENERAL ISSUES

Cemeteries are an expression of a community, including the varied cultural beliefs that make the community unique. Respecting the dead means extending that respect to their living descendants.[9]

Any cemetery worthy of restoration deserves a good plan for its refurbishment. The most effective master plans are those developed with input from the individuals interested in and authorized to care for the cemetery. The plan should:

1. Include performing an initial assessment of the cemetery's condition before any work is done and developing a list of cleanup and repair needs;

2. Outline which portion of the project requires professional expertise or materials;

3. Outline what can be done by untrained volunteers;

4. Include strategies for raising money to fund needed professional work and future maintenance requirements;

5. Address contacting descendants. If it is your own family's cemetery, consult other descendants before beginning work. If it is not your family's cemetery:
   a. make an effort to locate living heirs or descendants of the people buried in the cemetery being restored;
   b. obtain their permission for work you want to undertake; and
   c. invite their input regarding the restoration project.

[9] Texas Historical Commission, *Texas Preservation Guidelines: Preserving Historic Cemeteries.* Online. Internet. 22 September 2000. Available: http://www.thc.state.tx.us.

When your family or church cemetery is located on private property, you may have the implied right of access to the property to visit it. However, we strongly recommend that before crossing someone else's property, you first notify the current landowner that you want access and then reach a mutual agreement with the owner regarding frequency and means of access to the cemetery.

If you want to clean up and reclaim a cemetery that has been neglected for many years, it may be useful to contact other local groups or individuals in Georgia who have already been through the process for another cemetery. The restoration effort is usually more than a one-person job and you may benefit from learning how others have gone about getting the work done. To locate such groups, start by seeing if a cemetery book has been written about your county. Consult your local library or look in Ted Brooke's bibliography of recorded cemeteries, noted in Appendix A. Contact the author of any cemetery books you find to see if that person is aware of any cleanup projects done by people in your county, or even previous projects on the cemetery you're interested in. Be sure to ask if there is someone you might contact about those undertakings.

Additionally, contact local historical societies to see if they know of any cemetery cleanup efforts. Finally, contact the preservation planner for your county's regional development center, who may have knowledge of cemetery projects in your part of the state and may also inquire of their board members about cemetery cleanups in the board members' hometowns. If you need information about which RDC region your county is in and the preservation planner, you may contact the Community Planning Coordinator in the Historic Preservation Division office, 404.656.2840, or refer to the RDC map and links to RDC offices at http://www.cviog.uga.edu/Projects/gainfo/regionmaps/rdc.htm.

If the cemetery you want to clean up contains American Indian burials, then it will be necessary to contact the Georgia Council on American Indian Concerns and request their guidance in any activities that may impact the Indian graves. Contact their representative at the Parks, Recreation & Historic Sites Division of the Georgia Department of Natural Resources, 2 Martin Luther King Jr. Drive, Suite 1352, East Tower, Atlanta, GA 30334; phone 404.656.2770.

In the restoration planning process, you should consider what group of individuals will be responsible for seeing that maintenance is continued in the future. This is often a thorny issue because the responsibility for maintenance must be carried on indefinitely, beyond the lifespans of those who initiate the idea, and it will require money as well as labor. If the cemetery is owned by a church, its long-term care may be assured if the current congregation assumes that responsibility and passes on the responsibility to the younger generation of church members. Forming a non-profit "friends of the cemetery" group is often a successful way to deal with maintenance issues. For information on how a family, church, or other individuals can form a non-profit cemetery care group, see the section titled **FUNDING A RESTORATION PROJECT,** page 40.

RESTORATION PLAN – SPECIFIC STEPS

Step 1. Before any work is done, look over the entire cemetery and assess its overall condition. Nothing should be moved, removed, or cut down before it is recorded in its current position. Are there many or only a few markers that need repair? Is there a lot of plant debris to be removed? Can it be done by hand easily? Are there trees threatening grave markers that might need to be taken down? Does the fencing need repair or does a fence need to be installed? Are there soil erosion problems that need to be addressed? Make notes about your observations. They will be the basis for planning what is to be done and how to direct your volunteer labor.

Step 2. Using paper with a printed grid or graph paper, sketch a map as close to scale as possible showing the cemetery boundary lines and features. Distances can be measured using a hand-held GPS unit. Another handy piece of equipment for calculating lengthy boundary distances is a measuring wheel, a device with a long handle connected to a wheel with a mechanism that measures the distance the wheel is rolled. You may be able to borrow a measuring wheel from the local high school (used to measure distances on the sports field), a real estate office, or perhaps the local police. Measuring a small cemetery's boundaries might be done by first calculating how many normal steps it takes you to walk the distance of a yard. Then walk each side of the cemetery, keeping count of your steps. Divide that total by the number of your strides to make a yard and you will have the boundary line's distance in yards. Then convert the distance into feet by multiplying by three.

On the map, record the location and orientation of visible graves and other landscape features, such as walking paths, large trees, walls, and fences. Use a compass to determine which direction is north and mark a north arrow appropriately on the map for directional reference. (See a sample map on page 57.) Also, a GPS unit might be useful to record the exact location of each grave.

Note the county name and the cemetery's relative position to the nearest town (e.g., N, SE, NW) on the map. Write a clear set of directions to the cemetery from a permanent beginning point in the nearest town, such as the intersection of two main streets. It is important to use landmarks that aren't apt to be lost from the landscape, such as a stand of trees that might die or be cut down. Identify main highway(s) and distances. Be sure to date all of your documentation.

Step 3. Make a photographic record of all graves, markers, coping around graves, fencing, monuments, and other landscape features. Be sure to keep a photo log of the subject of each exposure and key the photos into the map you have sketched. You can use a simple table like the one below:

Film Exp #	Map Feature #	Description	View Direction	Date/ Photographer
1	12	John Doe Head stone + Foot stone	Side View Facing South	11/10/01 Beth Johnson
2	8	Graveyard Entry Gate	Front View	1/2/02 Roy Mason
3				

Step 4. Study professional information on historic burial customs and plants that were popular in the past for use around graves. That will help you make decisions about which plants and other items should be left in place and which should be removed (for information on plantings and customs, see section entitled **PROFESSIONAL GUIDANCE**, page 36). Be aware that equipment such as weedeaters, lawnmowers, and even metal garden tools used too close to stones may scar the stones, leaving them vulnerable to corrosion and breakage. Read about the effects of herbicides on stone in order to make good decisions about which chemicals to use, if any, in weed management around grave markers. Lynette Strangstad in her book, <u>A Graveyard Preservation Primer</u>, advises against using commercial herbicides because "virtually all contain salts or acids that are damaging to most stone, particularly marble and limestone."[10]

Plan the initial part of the cleanup for the winter months when vegetation naturally dies back. Remove dead trees, fallen tree limbs, leaf litter, and any shrubbery or trees threatening to damage a marker. The next phase of cleanup might be scheduled for the spring when it is easier to see plants as they leaf out and bloom. Then you can distinguish between ornamental plants intentionally placed to decorate a grave and weeds that should be removed.

Consider removing large trees that may topple or break grave markers.

---

[10] Lynette Strangstad, *A Graveyard Preservation Primer* (Walnut Creek: AltaMira Press, 1995), 48.

Step 5. Using information published by experts on the proper tools and cleaning solutions, plan clean up activities using appropriate equipment for specific jobs. It is essential to get advice from professionals about tombstone cleaning. Utilizing researched, safe cleaning/restoration materials and methods will ensure that further inadvertent damage does not result from well-intentioned volunteer efforts. For example, it may be best to use only clear water and a soft bristled brush (no wire bristles) to clean tombstones. Other cleaning solutions may corrode the stone (e.g., muriatic acid). Most common household cleaners should be avoided (e.g., bleach). The products suggested by several recognized experts are:

- non-ionic detergents used by conservation specialists such as Triton X-100 or Igepal
- Photo-Flo, a product used in photography
- Vulpex, also a professional conservation product
- household ammonia, mixed 1 part ammonia to 4 parts water[11]

Protect stones from unintentional damage by using wooden or plastic gardening tools rather than those made of metal. Refer to publications listed in this section for specific guidance on chemicals, tools, and methods.

Step 6. Prepare a written plan for the clean up, delineating jobs to be done by volunteers and those that require hiring an expert. Keep in mind that various parts of the project may need to be done at different times, taking advantage of good weather, seasons when vegetation dies back, and times when insects or snakes are less of a problem. Plan to bring trash receptacles, benches or lawn chairs for taking a break from the work, and plenty of drinking water.

[11] Ibid., p. 63; and Chicora Foundation, "General Guide to Cleaning Products" in *Cemetery Preservation: Making Good Choices* (Columbia, South Carolina: Chicora Foundation, Inc.)

Step 7. On the actual workdays, use your written plan to direct activities. Remind all volunteers of the respect to be shown while working around gravestones. Explain their specific jobs and the information you have gathered regarding plantings and funerary items that should be left in place. Review the proper kinds of tools to be used and why. Also for the volunteers' information, let them know landowner permission has been obtained and that descendants have been contacted for input on the project.

Step 8. Prepare a standard form for all recording activities so the information gathered will be consistent. Give copies to the volunteers working on that portion of the project. The recorded information should include the type of stone (e.g., marble, granite, slate, field stone), marker style (die on base, column, tablets, box tomb, bedstead), dimensions, and inscriptions exactly as they appear. Be sure everyone is equipped with a tape measure.

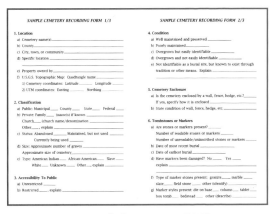

See sample form, pages 54-56.

Consider giving the volunteers advance training in identifying types of stone used for markers, marker styles, and how to accurately record inscriptions. You might consider working up a "cheat sheet" for volunteers to use in the field, with pictures/drawings and names of common marker styles and ways to distinguish stone types. Alert them that occasionally the stone carver's name may be found on the base of a headstone, at or below the ground level.

Be sure that all information about each stone is keyed into its location marked on your map and to the proper film exposure number on the photo log. The recording might be done by one set of volunteers while others are participating in the clean up activities. For more about recording techniques, see <u>Recording Historic Cemeteries: A Guide for Historical Societies and Genealogists</u> by the Chicora Foundation, <u>A Graveyard Preservation Primer</u> by Lynette Strangstad, or <u>South Carolina's Historic Cemeteries: A Preservation Handbook</u> by Susan H. McGahee and Mary W. Edmonds (see publication information in Appendix A).

Avoid rubbing chalk on the lettering to see it better – some experts say chalk will not easily come off and can attract dirt and other destructive material onto the stone, hastening the stone's corrosion. Taping paper on the stone and rubbing crayon, pencil lead, or chalk on the paper is less of a threat to the stone. However, the tape's adhesive may linger and attract dirt, which in turn leads to the stone's deterioration. In addition, some old stones might already be in a weakened condition and the pressure of rubbing could break off pieces or snap the whole marker. Professionals suggest a better technique is to use a mirror to reflect sunlight onto the stone or a flashlight, experimenting with the angle of the light until the inscription is more easily read.

Step 9. Organize the information collected during the workdays, including the map, photos, locational descriptions, and recording forms. Write up a short narrative description of the work performed in your project – it will be of particular benefit to future caretakers of the cemetery. Note how volunteers were recruited and the kinds of support received from the community such as donated materials or services used during the workdays. Arrange for the safekeeping of this project information, where it will be accessible by other interested parties.

There are several publications available that explain the range of issues to be considered such as recording techniques, cleaning methods, and how to fund a project, as well as provide lists of other resources that may be helpful. A Graveyard Preservation Primer by Strangstad, cited above, is an excellent guide. A short but helpful publication is Recording Historic Cemeteries: A Guide for Historical Societies and Genealogists by the Chicora Foundation, Inc., mentioned above. In twelve pages, it gives the basics on supplies, tools, and methods, mapping the cemetery, items your project should cover, and photographic examples of various tombstone types. For a copy, contact Chicora Foundation at P.O. Box 8664, 861 Arbutus Drive, Columbia, SC 29202-8664 or go to their Web site at www.chicora.org.

Another good source to consult for guidance with a number of issues is Florida's Historic Cemeteries: A Preservation Handbook, by Sharyn Thompson. Even though it was written using Florida cemeteries as examples, the concepts it discusses are applicable anywhere. South Carolina's Department of Archives and History also offers for sale South Carolina's Historic Cemeteries: A Preservation Handbook and a videotape entitled Lest We Forget: Preserving Historic Cemeteries, which summarizes guidelines for recording, preserving, and maintaining historic cemeteries. This tape features Lynette Strangstad and can be purchased from SCETV Marketing, Box 11000, Columbia, SC 29211, phone 800.553.7752.

REPAIRING TOMBSTONES, FENCES, AND CEMETERY LANDSCAPE FEATURES

The work required in your cemetery may include repair or replacement of tombstones, fences, walkways, and cemetery landscapes. Long-neglected graveyard architectural and landscape elements should first be carefully documented before any repair is undertaken. Then the items most threatened with destruction can be given priority.

Stone marker repair is a new, still-evolving craft and is best left to specialized professionals. There is not yet a consensus of opinion even among experts as to the best repair materials or

techniques. Some tombstone repairs have failed after a period of time and much can be learned from others' trials. For an example of what *not* to do, see the National Park Service Ft. Bragg Gravestone Restoration Project at www.cr.nps.gov/seac/seac.htm.

If you believe some stones require repair, you will likely need to hire a professional to do the actual work. However, it will be worthwhile to first read some of the published information on current methods and materials to be better informed when discussing your needs with a consultant. Examples of consultants who do this type of work are the Chicora Foundation, located in South Carolina, and Lynette Strangstad at Stone Faces and Sacred Spaces, located in Wisconsin (see Appendix A for contact information).

PROFESSIONAL GUIDANCE

Professional marker conservationists, Linwood Cemetery, Columbus, GA.

While much of the work in a cemetery can be done by volunteers, guidance from professionals will be valuable in many aspects of your project. Someone who has seen the results of a poorly planned project can attest to the fact that even clearing overgrown vegetation should be done carefully in order not to impact fragile grave markers or destroy foliage that was purposefully planted to decorate a grave plot. Experts will caution that herbicides and pesticides could have harmful effects on tombstone material and plantings. In the National Trust for Historic Preservation's bulletin titled "Preservation of Historic Burial Grounds," the author notes that lawn mowers are a primary cause of damage to historic markers. Burial grounds from certain historic periods were not closely mown like modern cemeteries are today. So it may be more historically correct and certainly is more protective to grave markers to adopt a less manicured approach to cemetery grounds maintenance.

Consideration should also be given to whether an archaeological survey is needed. An archaeologist would not dig up any graves but would find out information that is not otherwise available. Such an investigation could accurately define the cemetery boundaries, by documenting the location of unmarked graves, and reveal other interesting landscape features of the graveyard that are no longer visible to the untrained eye.

Other experts needed might include a historian, horticulturist, or landscape architect, who may be able to shed additional light on how cemeteries of a particular era were landscaped and arranged. Enlist assistance from someone familiar with traditional plantings from the cemetery's era so that historic vegetation purposefully put there is

Identify and save historic plants.

not inadvertently removed during cleanup. This should be one of the first steps taken when planning a cemetery restoration or cleanup. For assistance in identifying historic plantings, you could contact the local cooperative extension service for a list of their master gardeners. A master gardener may be able to provide you with a plant guide to take into the cemetery for identifying what is still there. Be sure to remember that some vegetation is not visible in winter or may only flower in early spring, so the identification of plants may need to be done over several months of the year.

Enlist a master gardener's help.

Additionally, specialists can give vital guidance in respecting historical burial practices that may be represented in the subject cemetery. Various cultural and religious groups throughout time have had distinctly different ways of commemorating their dead. Cemetery traditions that we see practiced now may have been different in the past. Other traditions may not even be recognizable as formal burial customs to some of us from our 21st century perspectives. For example, scholars who have studied historic burial customs of black Americans in the South have found that graves were often decorated with seashells and other personal items or utensils, many of which were broken. An observation from the 1880s of a cemetery in Columbia, South Carolina, records this practice.

When a Negro dies, some article or utensil, or more than one, is thrown upon his grave; moreover it is broken. If you go through a dilapidated weed-grown graveyard which straggles in and out of the hollows on a side hill covering the high bluffs along the river, you will see some very strange examples of this mortuary custom. Nearly every grave has bordering or thrown upon it a few bleached sea-shells of a dozen different kinds . . . mingled with these is a most curious collection of broken crockery and glassware. On the large graves are laid broken pitchers, soap-dishes, lamp chimneys, tureens, coffee-cups, sirup jugs, all sorts of ornamental vases, cigar boxes, gun-locks, tomato cans, teapots, flower-pots, bits of stucco, plaster images, . . . and other kitchen articles.[12]

Burial customs vary broadly and should be respected.

---

[12] Simon J. Bronner, ed., *Folklife Studies from the Gilded Age: Object, Rite, and Custom in Victorian America* (Ann Arbor: UMI Research Press, 1987), 168.

Debris on a grave may be deceiving.

If you are cleaning up an old, neglected cemetery, broken crockery or random seashells may look like debris that should be cleaned off a grave and thrown away. However, as the example above demonstrates, these kinds of items may have been purposefully put there and ought to be left in place. You should approach any cemetery cleanup or restoration with knowledge of and respect for the interment customs of the people who buried their dead there. An archaeologist or historian could help determine what burial practices likely were in use by the people represented in the cemetery and during the era when the cemetery was active. For a list of archaeology/historic preservation consulting firms in Georgia, contact the Historic Preservation Division at 404.656.2840 and speak to someone in the Archaeology Services Unit. To read more about African-American cemeteries, see information posted online by the Chicora Foundation at www.sciway.net/hist/chicora/gravematters.html.

In addition to gaining knowledge to guide your restoration efforts, you need to be aware of possible hazards in historic burial places. According to John Konefes and Michael McGee in their article, "Old Cemeteries, Arsenic, and Health Safety,"[13] a little-known danger that can lurk in old cemeteries is from arsenic. Use of embalming fluids containing arsenic became very widespread during the Civil War and continued until about 1910. Konefes and McGee explain that arsenic is toxic and does not degrade over time. The wood and metal materials of coffins do corrode, allowing the arsenic from human remains to seep into the soil and/or groundwater. Arsenic poisoning can result from ingestion, inhalation, or skin contact. This does not necessarily require contact with a corpse,

---

[13] John L. Konefes and Michael K. McGee, "Old Cemeteries, Arsenic, and Health Safety," in *Dangerous Places: Health, Safety, and Archaeology*, ed. David A. Poirier and Kenneth L. Feder (Westport, Connecticut: Bergin & Garvey, 2000), 127.

but may happen merely by handling objects containing the arsenic compounds or inhaling contaminated dust that has settled on objects such as work clothing.[14] When cleanup efforts will entail taking out underbrush and trees from grave plots, or otherwise disturbing the ground or nearby water, it may be prudent to contact an archaeological or environmental consultant regarding the possibility of toxic substances being present in the area.

FUNDING A RESTORATION PROJECT

Our office has no knowledge of a source of funding for cemetery restoration. It is appropriate for family members or a church group to finance the hiring of an expert in restoration to perform the needed professional work. However, below is a list of other ideas for funding sources. Note that it will most likely be easier for a non-profit organization, rather than an individual, to get grant money for cemetery restoration work.

- ◆ Form a cemetery "friends" group to solicit donations for the cemetery's restoration, which may be organized as a non-profit, tax-exempt entity under the Internal Revenue Service Code section 501(c)(3) definition. See The Association for Gravestone Studies' Guide to Forming A "Cemetery Friends" Organization, published by the Association for Gravestone Studies, 278 Main Street, Suite 207, Greenfield, MA 01301; http://www.gravestonestudies.org.

- ◆ Look for other family cemeteries in your area; perhaps representatives from each cemetery would be interested in coming together to form an association to share planning and funding strategies.

- ◆ If there is an existing non-profit organization nearby that is interested, the cemetery restoration could become the project of one of its committees.

---

[14] Ibid., pp. 132-133.

◆ Descendants of the people buried in the cemetery may have an interest in contributing.

◆ Even local funeral homes or monument companies may want to participate when community support for the cemetery project is demonstrated.

◆ Another avenue to pursue is to contact the Chamber of Commerce, historical society, or the Main Street Program manager if the community has that status, to inquire about possible partners in a cemetery project. Their contacts and work in the community might be helpful.

However, often a private fund-raising effort by the family or a historical society is the quickest way to get the necessary money.

The Foundation Center, 50 Hurt Plaza, Suite 150, Atlanta, GA 30303-2914, phone 404.880.0094, is a library devoted to information on funding sources for all types of projects. They maintain a database on foundations and corporate giving programs and may be a good starting place to research possible financial support for your cemetery project. Along with other helpful seminars, the center offers free weekly orientation sessions, *Grantseeking Basics: An Orientation to the Funding Research Process*, to explain how to use their resources and go about looking for funding. Registration is necessary for the free sessions; call 404.880.0095 or register online at their Web site, http://www.fdncenter.org.

Local Governments

Local governments allocate money in their budgets for the larger municipal or city cemeteries, and they have the authority to allocate funds for the upkeep of abandoned cemeteries, as defined under the Abandoned Cemeteries and Burial Grounds law. Alternatively, they may be willing to work with a local society on joint fund raising activities. As cited earlier in this publication, the

Abandoned Cemeteries and Burial Grounds law authorizes county and city governments to "preserve and protect any cemetery which the county or municipality determines has been abandoned or is not being maintained and to expend public money in connection therewith."[15] The law defines "preserve and protect" as to "keep safe from destruction, peril, and other adversity,"[16]

An unofficial opinion issued by the Georgia Attorney General's office in October 1999 provides another source for assistance in maintaining abandoned cemeteries that a county or municipality has acquired. The opinion says that "persons sentenced to community service may properly be utilized to assist counties or municipalities in preserving and protecting abandoned cemeteries or burial grounds."[17] This means that a city or county may use inmates or those on probation as supervised labor to help with cleanup in abandoned cemeteries. This ruling could contribute substantially to a local government's ability to take on the responsibility of acquiring and maintaining such a cemetery. A concerned community group or individual could bring this ruling to the attention of their local governing authorities when lobbying for the city to take over an abandoned cemetery. This opinion can be found at the Georgia Attorney General's Web site, www.law.state.ga.us, or a copy can be requested from the State of Georgia Law Library, 244 Washington Street, Atlanta, GA 30334, phone 404.656.3468. (See footnote for this opinion's reference information).

---

[15] Ga. Code § 36-72-3 (2001).
[16] Ga. Code § 36-72-2[9] (2001).
[17] Christopher S. Brasher, Senior Assistant Attorney General, "Georgia Attorney General's Unofficial Opinion U99-5, Re: Persons sentenced to community service may be utilized to assist counties or municipalities in preserving and protecting abandoned cemeteries or burial grounds" dated October 15, 1999.

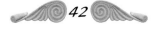

Georgia Department
of Natural Resources

Historic Preservation Division funding

HPD administers two grant programs, the Historic Preservation Fund and the Georgia Heritage grant program. The division annually receives funds from the National Park Service for Historic Preservation Fund grants, which are awarded on a 60/40 matching basis. However, a recent memorandum from the state attorney general's office states that, according to the Georgia Constitution, no money shall be taken from the public treasury in aid of any religious denomination or sectarian institution. This means that church-owned cemeteries cannot receive these grants. Further, this program usually does not cover private family cemetery restoration because applications must be submitted by local governments who have Certified Local Government status, the subject property must be eligible for listing in the National Register of Historic Places, and the project must be for predevelopment, or survey and planning.

The Georgia Heritage grant program is a state-funded grant program designed to support development and predevelopment historic preservation projects only on properties that are eligible for the Georgia Register of Historic Places. Grant applicants must either be a local government or a non-profit organization. Cemetery cleanup falls into the category of routine maintenance and is therefore not eligible for this type of grant. However, a qualified applicant might be successful in securing this grant for restoration of retaining walls, steps, monuments, or markers, for example, in a Georgia Register-eligible cemetery.

For more information about these grants, you may contact the grants coordinator at HPD by phone at 404.656.2840 or through our Web site, http://www.gashpo.org.

Maintenance of a cemetery is a long-term responsibility.

4

PROTECTING A CEMETERY

MAINTENANCE

Maintenance of a cemetery requires a substantial commitment from the people who are interested in its care. There are two main issues to consider: first, the long-term responsibility for actual physical maintenance; and second, the continuing need for funding to pay for maintenance. While it is commendable to perform the initial cleanup of a neglected cemetery and restoration of grave markers, it is equally important to make long-range plans for the continued care necessary in the face of progressive deterioration from natural forces. An entity such as the local historical society or other interested group would be a good candidate to take on this responsibility.

Long-term care is also necessary to deter vandalism and theft. Cleaning up a cemetery the first time and then allowing it to become neglected again may, in fact, be worse than not cleaning it up at all. After the cleanup, the markers and other cemetery items can be seen more easily. Then looters and vandals are alerted by obvious lack of continued attention. They know they can easily steal grave markers or desecrate graves if the cemetery is not being monitored. To avoid or minimize occurrences of destructive activity in the cemetery, set up a plan for on-going regular inspections of the cemetery and clearly assign responsibility for the inspections.

LOOTING AND VANDALISM

Another critical aspect of cemetery protection is that of security against vandals or looters, who may be drawn to a cemetery as discussed above. In recent years, mortuary art has been in great demand on the antiquities market. Tombstones and other grave markers, as well as ornate fencing, can be stolen and easily sold by looters. The maintenance plan for your cemetery should cover provisions for monitoring the grounds periodically, including photographs and a list of particularly vulnerable items to be checked for disturbance.

It is advisable to have the caretakers/owners of the cemetery meet with local law enforcement personnel to apprise them of the restoration effort, the value of the cemetery to the descendants and the community, and to request their advice about keeping it safe from criminal acts. Consider requesting that law enforcement officials add the cemetery to their regularly scheduled patrol.

It is important to protect cemeteries against vandals.

DEVELOPMENT THREATS

Help inform developers who may not know a cemetery exists on their property.

One of the major threats to cemeteries today is commercial and residential development. Often company officials and government agents are unfamiliar with local history and may not understand the value of what could be damaged or destroyed. Additionally, deed and tax records do not always indicate the presence of a cemetery on a tract of property, and the cemetery may not be readily visible because there are no markings or the vegetation is overgrown. In those instances, developers may not know a cemetery exists on their property.

The abandoned cemeteries law requires a permit for developing or changing the use of land on which a **"known"** cemetery is located. *This is why recording a cemetery in public documents is so important.* If the cemetery's existence is not noted in public records, then the abandoned cemeteries law may not provide any protection. However, protection is provided by the laws prohibiting disturbing human remains, and the developer may need to be apprised of those laws. (See Appendix B, 2001 Ga. Code § 31-21-6 and § 31-21-44).

Publicity can play a strong role in influencing someone to stop threatening or damaging a cemetery. Every moment counts when such a fragile resource is being desecrated. Even a few hours could be critical. If you have knowledge of someone preparing to use heavy equipment or begining other action that will adversely affect the cemetery, first attempt to stop the activity by notifying the developer of the cemetery's existence. Have photographs and documentation in hand about the cemetery as well as the relevant laws. Initiate the discussion with intent to inform, not badger, the parties involved. They may not be aware that the cemetery even exists. In the recent past, news articles have reported lawsuits being filed based on the deceptive practice of selling off land that had been, in actuality, dedicated for cemetery use without the purchaser being aware of that intended use.

If apprising the parties involved of possible graves in the area does not have the desired effect, then you may consider contacting law enforcement officials. Under Ga. Code § 31-21-6 (2001), anyone who believes human remains are being disturbed should contact their local police. In addition, the local newspaper may be interested if the cemetery continues to be threatened. Publicity implying that a new development may be atop or disturbing a cemetery could create enough public sentiment to convince the parties involved to protect the graves.

LAWS

While Georgia's laws place certain responsibilities on owners or operators of modern perpetual care cemeteries, there are no state laws that require the owner of a historic, non-perpetual care cemetery to provide for its upkeep, maintenance, or accessibility. The owner of a larger cemetery with public visibility and access may be subject to existing public safety laws; however, none of those laws specifically apply to cemeteries.

If a landowner or developer is proceeding with actions that threaten a cemetery, then you must be knowledgeable of the laws that do protect cemeteries in order to lodge a valid complaint with the local law enforcement officials. You should remember that county and municipal government personnel are sometimes unaware of rarely-used statutes and should be informed of them. No one likes to be blindsided.

Under Georgia law the following legal conditions and obligations prevail. (Emphasis provided by author.)

♦ No **known** cemetery, burial ground, human remains, or burial object shall be **knowingly** disturbed by the owner or occupier of the land on which the cemetery or burial ground is located for the purposes of developing or changing the use of any part of such land **unless a permit is first obtained from the governing authority . . . wherein the cemetery or burial ground is located** (Ga. Code § 36-72-4 (2001)).

♦ Any person who knowingly violates the permitting process of Ga. Code § 36-72-4 and is convicted shall be **guilty of misdemeanor of a high and aggravated nature,** shall be jailed for not more than six months, and shall pay a fine of not less than $5,000.00 for each gravesite disturbed. Anyone knowingly violating any other provision of Chapter 36-72 shall pay a fine of not more than $5,000.00 for each gravesite disturbed (Ga. Code § 36-72-16 (2001)).

♦ If you accidentally or inadvertently discover or expose human remains you **shall immediately notify* local law enforcement** (Ga. Code § 31-21-6[a] (2001)). The instance of the discovery or exposure must be investigated the same way a crime scene would be.

♦ If you know or have reason to believe that interred human remains have been or are being disturbed, destroyed, defaced, mutilated, removed, or exposed without a permit you **shall immediately notify* local law enforcement** (Ga. Code § 31-21-6[a] (2001)).

♦ No one can wantonly or maliciously remove dead bodies from any grave or place of interment or otherwise disturb the contents of any grave or place of interment (Ga. Code § 31-21-44[a] (2001)).

> * Notification given in compliance with these laws should be followed up in writing to insure that a record of the notice exists.

MOVING GRAVES

Whenever graves will be knowingly disturbed for the purpose of development or changing the use of the land, Georgia law requires that a permit be obtained from the municipality or county where the cemetery is located. The permit procedure, detailed in Ga. Code § 36-72-5, states that the application for a permit must include a legal title opinion as to ownership of the land, an archaeologist's report citing the number of graves present, survey by a registered surveyor showing boundaries of the cemetery based on the archaeologist's report, a plan prepared by a genealogist for identifying and notifying the descendants of those buried in the cemetery, and a proposal for mitigation or avoidance of the effects of the planned project on the cemetery. If the project proposes actually moving human remains, the permit application must set out the method of disinterment, place of reinterment, cost, and number of graves affected. (See a copy of this law in Appendix B.)

This law clearly emphasizes contacting descendants and considering their input before a grave is disturbed or moved. When the graves are aboriginal or American Indian, the law states the Council on American Concerns shall be consulted and notification given to known descendants as well as to any American Indian tribes that are culturally affiliated. (See contact information for this council in Appendix A.) Distributing notices in publications or posting inquiries on appropriate Internet sites can assist in locating relatives if courthouse records are not helpful. If a good faith effort has been made to notify heirs and none are forthcoming, then proof should be compiled that a reasonable search has been conducted. The following are examples of reports or articles in which the procedures undertaken to notify heirs and obtain permission are outlined.

◆ Nancy Creek Primitive Baptist Church Cemetery, DeKalb County, Georgia – report done by Darlene Roth, 1984, prior to MARTA construction that was going to require relocation of graves. Historical and archaeological investigations were done of the entire cemetery and, specifically, the impacted graves. A memorandum was issued outlining the notification procedures for next of kin. A copy of this report is on file at the DeKalb Historical Society, 101 East Court Square, Decatur, GA 30303, phone 404.373.1088.

◆ The efforts undertaken to move and reinter a lone Confederate soldier are discussed in an article by William R. Bowen, "The History and Archeology of a Civil War Soldier," <u>Atlanta Historical Journal</u> XXV (Fall 1981) 67-77. A copy of this journal is on file in the research library at the Atlanta History Center, 130 West Paces Ferry Road, NW, Atlanta, GA 30305-1366; phone 404.814.4040.

There has been at least one case where a well-meaning historical society moved a family cemetery from the grounds of a new factory to the city cemetery. When the heirs found out, they refused to give permission and the society was forced to move the burials back to the factory grounds. So seek permission first.

Small family cemeteries are often targeted for relocation in the face of development.

LIABILITY

Recently, the issue of liability has become pertinent because some cemeteries now are surrounded by suburban development such as housing projects, apartment complexes, or retail facilities. If someone is injured within the grounds of a historic cemetery, then the question arises as to who is liable for injuries or damage sustained. Does the owner of the surrounding land have any liability for the cemetery, even though legal practice recognizes easements rights that allow access by heirs to the cemetery? Do the descendants of those buried there have any responsibility, or does the group that has taken on maintaining the cemetery? These questions should be considered when you or your organization accepts the challenge and responsibility of restoring an old cemetery. We recommend getting the advice of an attorney if you are confronted with these kinds of problems.

SAMPLE CEMETERY RECORDING FORM

1. Location

   a) Cemetery name(s)_____

   b) County_____

   c) City, town, or community_____

   d) Specific location _____

   _____

   e) Property owned by_____

   f) U.S.G.S. Topographic Map: Quadrangle name _____

      1) Cemetery coordinates: Latitude _____ Longitude _____

      2) UTM coordinates: Easting _____ Northing _____

2. Classification

   a) Public: Municipal_____ County_____ State_____ Federal _____

   b) Private: Family_____ name(s) if known _____

      Church_____ church name/denomination _____

      Other_____ , explain _____

   c) Status: Abandoned _____ Maintained, but not used _____

              Currently being used _____

   d) Size: Approximate number of graves _____

      Approximate size of cemetery_____

   e) Type: American Indian_____ African-American_____ Slave _____

          White_____ Unknown _____ Other__, explain _____

3. Accessibility To Public

   a) Unrestricted _____

   b) Restricted_____ , explain _____

SAMPLE CEMETERY RECORDING FORM *(cont'd)*

4. Condition

    a) Well maintained and preserved _____

    b) Poorly maintained_____

    c) Overgrown but easily identifiable_____

    d) Overgrown and not easily identifiable_____

    e) Not identifiable as a burial site, but known to exist through tradition or other means. Explain _____

    _____

5. Cemetery Enclosure

    a) Is the cemetery enclosed by a wall, fence, hedge, etc.?_____

    If yes, specify how it is enclosed _____

    b) State condition of wall, fence, hedge, etc._____

6. Tombstones or Markers

    a) Are stones or markers present?_____

    Number of readable stones or markers _____

    Number of unreadable/uninscribed stones or markers _____

    b) Date of most recent burial _____

    c) Date of earliest burial_____

    d) Have markers been damaged? No _____ Yes _____

    explain _____

    _____

    f) Type of marker stones present: granite_____ marble _____

    slate_____ field stone _____ other (identify) _____

    g) Marker styles present: die on base____ column___ tablet____

    box tomb____ bedstead ____ other (describe)_____

SAMPLE CEMETERY RECORDING FORM (cont'd)

7. Note any hazards imperiling the cemetery's existence

_____

8. Has this cemetery been listed in an existing published or unpublished cemetery survey?_____ If yes, explain/identify publication _____

_____

9. Historical or other special significance of cemetery

_____

_____

10. Any other information pertinent to the cemetery

_____

_____

11. Please attach a list of individuals buried in this cemetery, including inscriptions on tombstones and dimensions of each marker. Sketch a map showing the layout of the graves and key the inscription information to each stone's location on your sketch map.

Date_____
Survey form submitted by_____
Organization_____
Address_____
E-mail_____
Telephone _____
Thank You!

56

SAMPLE CEMETERY SKETCH MAP

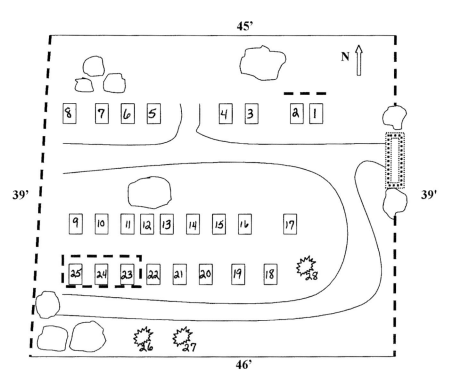

WORKS CITED

Bronner, Simon J., ed. *Folklife Studies from the Gilded Age: Object, Rite, and Custom in Victorian America.* Ann Arbor: UMI Research Press, 1987.

Brooke, Ted O. *The Cemetery Book: Cemetery Preservation, Restoration & Recording.* Atlanta: The Georgia Genealogical Society, 1989.

Chicora Foundation, Inc. "General Guide to Cleaning Products." In *Cemetery Preservation: Making Good Choices.* Columbia, South Carolina: Chicora Foundation, Inc., 2001.

Council on American Indian Concerns. *Artifact Collecting and the Law in Georgia: What's Legal and What's Not.* Atlanta: Council on American Indian Concerns, n.d.

Hinkel, Daniel F. *Pindar's Georgia Real Estate Law and Procedure With Forms.* 5th ed. Vol. 1. Norcross, Georgia: The Harrison Company, 1998.

Konefes, John L. and Michael K. McGee. "Old Cemeteries, Arsenic, and Health Safety." *In Dangerous Places: Health, Safety, and Archaeology,* ed. David A. Poirier and Kenneth L. Feder. Westport, Connecticut: Bergin & Garvey, 2000.

Official Code of Georgia §36-72-1 *et seq.* Retrieved online at http://www.georgia.gov, July 2002.

Potter, Elisabeth Walton and Beth M. Boland. *National Register Bulletin, No. 41: Guidelines for Evaluating and Registering Cemeteries and Burial Places.* Washington: U.S. Department of the Interior, National Park Service, 1992.

Shrimpton, Rebecca H., ed. National Register Bulletin: How to Apply the *National Register Criteria for Evaluation*. Washington: U.S. Department of the Interior, National Park Service, 1997.

Strangstad, Lynette. *A Graveyard Preservation Primer*. Walnut Creek, California: AltaMira Press, 1995.

State of Georgia, Department of Law. Attorney General Opinion U99-5. Atlanta: Department of Law, State of Georgia, 1999.

Texas Historical Commission. *Texas Preservation Guidelines: Preserving Historic Cemeteries*. Texas Historical Commission. Online. Internet. 22 September 2000.

GEORGIA CEMETERIES

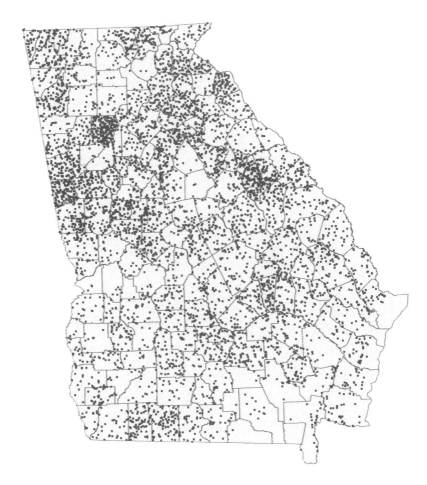

Approximately 5548 known cemeteries were marked on U.S.G.S. topographic quadrangle maps for GA as of 1970.

APPENDIX   A

<u>HISTORIC CEMETERIES: INFORMATION SOURCES</u>

This appendix comprises resources compiled as of **July 2002**. Beyond that date, this information may not be current.

TABLE OF CONTENTS

Historic Cemeteries: Information Sources

HISTORIC CEMETERIES: INFORMATION SOURCES

PUBLICATIONS

Baker, J. Joanne and Daniel Farber with Anne G. Giesicke. "Recording Cemetery Data." <u>Markers: The Annual Journal of the Association for Gravestone Studies</u> 1 (1980): 99-117.

Bowen, William R. "The History and Archeology of a Civil War Soldier." <u>Atlanta Historical Journal</u> XXV (Fall 1981): 67-77. Discusses the efforts undertaken to move and reinter a lone Confederate soldier.

Brooke, Ted O., ed. <u>Cemetery Preservation, Restoration & Recording</u>. Atlanta: The Georgia Genealogical Society, 1989. Guide for recording cemetery information.

Georgia Cemetery Directory and Bibliography of <u>Georgia Cemetery Reference Sources</u>. Marietta, GA: Ted O. Brooke, 1985. Guide to previously published cemetery records.

Coombs, Diane Williams. <u>Early Gravestone Art in Georgia and South Carolina</u>. Athens, Georgia: University of Georgia Press, 1986.

Crawford, Sybil F. <u>The Association for Gravestone Studies' Guide to Forming A "Cemetery Friends" Organization</u>. Greenfield, MA: The Association for Gravestone Studies, 1995. 278 Main St., Suite 207, Greenfield, MA 01301.

Dickens, Jr., Roy S. and Robert L. Blakely. "Preliminary Report on Archaeological Investigations in Oakland Cemetery, Atlanta, Georgia." <u>The Conference on Historic Site Archaeology Papers,</u>

XIII (1978) 286-314. A copy is at the Atlanta History Center; is a good example of the research involved in establishing the dimensions of a cemetery and the actual existence of unmarked graves.

Hinkel, Daniel F. "§ 8-44.1 Burial and cemetery easements." <u>Pindar's Georgia Real Estate Law and Procedure With Forms</u>, Fifth Edition, Volume 1. Norcross, GA: The Harrison Company, 1998.

Historic Preservation Division, Department of Natural Resources, 156 Trinity Avenue, SW, Suite 101, Atlanta, GA 30303-3600; phone 404.656.2840; http://www.gashpo.org. Publications available:

Georgia's Regional Preservation Planning Services

The Georgia Heritage Grant Program

Keeping Historic Preservation in the Public Eye

Writing the History of Your Community

The National Register of Historic Places: Recognizing and Preserving Our Historic Places

Professional Qualifications Standards: History, Archaeology, Architectural History, and Historic Architecture.

Jones, Mary-Ellen. <u>Photographing Tombstones: Equipment and Techniques</u>, American Association for State and Local History Technical Leaflet #92. Nashville, TN: American Association for State and Local History (1977).

Mayer, Lance R. "The Care of Old Cemeteries and Gravestones." <u>Markers: The Annual Journal of the Association of Gravestone Studies</u>, 1 (1980): 119-141.

McGahee, Susan and Mary Edmonds. <u>South Carolina's Historic Cemeteries: A Preservation Handbook</u>. Columbia, SC: South Carolina Department of Archives and History, 1997. To purchase, contact the SC Dept. of Archives and History, http://www.state.sc.us/scdah.

National Park Service, U. S. Department of Interior, Cultural Resources, Interagency Resources Division. <u>National Register Bulletin 41: Guidelines for Evaluating and Registering Cemeteries and Burial Places</u>. Washington, D.C.: U. S. Department of Interior. P. O. Box 37127, Washington, D.C. 20013-7127. Also available online at http://www.cr.nps.gov/nr/publications/bulletins/cem.htm

Also see the National Park Service's series of <u>Preservation Briefs</u> which address technical information on common preservation and repair problems concerning specific materials such as stone, masonry, and brick.

National Trust for Historic Preservation, P. O. Box 96056, Washington, DC 20077-7272; phone 202.588.6296. Publications can be ordered from Preservation Books, National Trust for Historic Preservation, http://www.nthpbooks.org.

"Preservation of Historic Burial Grounds" by Lynette Strangstad. Information Series #76 National Trust for Historic Preservation, Item #2I76, 1993. $6.00

"Organizing Volunteers for Preservation Projects" by Judith WinterBell. Tips for carrying out a successful preservation project using a volunteer workforce and limited funds. National Trust for Historic Preservation, Item #2I09, 1993. $15.00

"Quest for Funds Revisited: A Fund-Raising Kit." by Joe Breiteneicher. National Trust for Historic Preservation, Item #2I75, 1998. $6.00

"Using Professional Consultants in Preservation." by Ellen Beasley. National Trust for Historic Preservation, Item #2I26, 2001. $6.00

South Carolina Department of Archives & History. <u>South Carolina's Historic Cemeteries: A Preservation Handbook</u>. Columbia, SC: South Carolina Department of Archives and History, 1997. P. O. Box 11669, Columbia, SC 29211; phone 803.734.8590; fax 803.734.8820.

Videotape entitled *Lest We Forget: Preserving Historic Cemeteries*, which summarizes guidelines for recording, preserving, and maintaining historic cemeteries; can be purchased from SCETV Marketing, Box 11000, Columbia, SC 29211, phone 800.553.7752. Order by using this videotape's catalog number, 196-000.

Strangstad, Lynette. <u>A Graveyard Preservation Primer</u>. Sponsored by The Association for Gravestone Studies. Nashville: American Association for State and Local History, 1988. 126 pages, paperback, $19.95. Available from Alta Mira Press, 2455 Teller Road, Thousand Oaks, CA 91320, phone 805.499.9774; fax 805.499.0871; http://www.altamirapress.com

Thompson, Sharyn. <u>Florida's Historic Cemeteries: A Preservation Handbook</u>. Tallahassee, Florida: Historic Tallahassee Preservation Board, 1989. For copy availability, contact The Center for Historic Cemeteries Preservation, P. O. Box 6296, Tallahassee, FL 32314.

Trinkley, Michael. Chicora Foundation, Inc., P. O. Box 8664, 861 Arbutus Drive, Columbia, SC 29202-8664; phone 803.787.6910; http://www.chicora.org.

Recording Historic Cemeteries: A Guide for Historical Societies and Genealogists. 12 pp. wire stitched. This booklet focuses on why and how to record historic cemeteries and graveyards. It provides essential advice for those beginning cemetery preservation projects. ISBN 1-58317-045-6 $2.00

Grave Matters: The Preservation of African-American Cemeteries. 16 pp.wire stitched. Explores the unique and exciting history of African-American cemeteries and how they can be easily damaged or destroyed by development or a lack of understanding. Suggests ways that this heritage can be preserved for future generations. ISBN 1-58317-008-1 $1.00

ORGANIZATIONS, AGENCIES, OTHER

Association for Gravestone Studies, 278 Main Street, Suite 207, Greenfield, MA 01301; phone 413.772.0836; http://www.gravestonestudies.org

Atlanta History Center, 130 West Paces Ferry Road, NW, Atlanta, GA 30305-1366; main phone 404.814.4000; research library 404.814.4040; http://www.atlantahistorycenter.com

Brooke, Ted O., 2055 Foster Drive, Cumming, GA 30040.

The Center for Historic Cemeteries Preservation, P. O. Box 6296, Tallahassee, FL 32314; phone 850.877.9014. Sharyn Thompson, a cemetery consultant, established the center to further the study and preservation of historic burial sites; her publications include a bibliography on historic African American and African Caribbean cemeteries and Florida's Historic Cemeteries: A Preservation Handbook.

Chicora Foundation, Inc., P. O. Box 8664, 861 Arbutus Drive, Columbia, SC 29202-8664; phone 803.787.6910; http://www.chicora.org. This is a consulting firm that offers a wide range of services and information relating to cemetery preservation.

Council on American Indian Concerns, 2 Martin Luther King Jr. Drive, Suite 1352 East Tower, Atlanta, GA 30334; phone 404.656.2770; http://www.ganet.org/indcouncil

DeKalb Historical Society, 101 East Court Square, Decatur, GA 30303, phone 404.373.1088; http://www.dekalbhistory.org

The Foundation Center, 50 Hurt Plaza, Suite 150, Atlanta, GA 30303-2914. This is a library of funding sources for all types of projects. Phone 404.880.0094; http://www.fdncenter.org

Georgia Archaeological Site File, University of Georgia, 110 Riverbend Road, Athens, GA 30602-4702; phone 706.542.8738; http://shapiro.anthro.uga.edu/GASF

Georgia Department of Archives and History, 330 Capitol Avenue, Atlanta, GA 30334; phone 404.656.2393; http://www.sos.state.ga.us/archives

Georgia Department of Transportation, 5025 New Peachtree Road, Chamblee, GA 30341; phone 770.986.1366; http://www.dot.state.ga.us. Contact this agency to have cemetery information added to their county highway maps.

Georgia Geologic Survey, 19 Martin Luther King, Jr., Drive, Atlanta, GA 30334; phone 404.656.3214. Contact this agency to purchase United States Geologic Survey (U.S.G.S.) maps of Georgia.

Georgia Historical Society – administers the current historic marker program. 501 Whitaker Street, Savannah, GA 31401; phone 912.651.2125; http://www.georgiahistory.com

Georgia Historic Marker Program – contact the Georgia Historical Society at address above.

Historic Preservation Division, Georgia Department of Natural Resources, 156 Trinity Avenue, S.W., Suite 101, Atlanta, GA 30303-3600, phone 404.656.2840; http://www.gashpo.org

South Carolina Department of Archives & History, Publications, P. O. Box 11669, Columbia, SC 29211; phone 803.734.8590; fax 803.734.8820; http://www.state.sc.us/scdah

Strangstad, Lynette, cemetery preservation consultant. Stone Faces and Sacred Spaces, P. O. Box 59, Mineral Point, WI 53565; phone 608.987.3222.

The Surveying and Mapping Society of Georgia (SAMSOG), P. O. Box 778, Douglasville, GA 30133-1272; phone 770.489.1440; http://www.samsog.org

R. J. Taylor, Jr. Foundation, a foundation trust to provide for the preservation and publication of genealogical information. Written correspondence should be addressed to SunTrust Bank, Atlanta, R. J. Taylor, Jr. Foundation, P. O. Box 4655, MC 221, Atlanta, GA 30302. Information is also available at their Web site: http://www.taylorfoundation.org.

U.S. Forest Service, 1755 Cleveland Highway, Gainesville, GA 30501; phone 770.536.0541; http://www.fs.fed.us/conf/

WEB SITES

African-American cemeteries information:
http://www.sciway.net/hist/chicora/gravematters.html.

African American Cemeteries Online: http://www.prairiebluff.com

Archival repositories in Georgia: http://www.soga.org/gar.html - On this site, the Society of Georgia Archivists maintains a list of all the archival repositories in Georgia.

Association for Gravestone Studies:
http://www.gravestonestudies.org - This association was founded to further the study and preservation of gravestones. It is an international organization; offers membership, publications, conferences, and other resources.

Cemetery maintenance and protection:
http://www.ctgravestones.com - Guidance on cemetery matters from the Connecticut Gravestone Network.

Cemetery preservation: http://www.potifos.com/cemeteries.html - Numerous links to resources on cemetery history and preservation, some of which are listed separately below.

Chicora Foundation, Inc.: http://www.chicora.org - Non-profit organization in South Carolina with the mission of preserving the archaeological, historical and cultural resources of the Carolinas; publications offer good general guidance on cemetery preservation issues.

Georgia Archaeological Site File:
http://shapiro.anthro.uga.edu/GASF

Georgia Historical Society: http://www.georgiahistory.com - Georgia Historical Society administers the historical marker program.

Georgia state laws: http://www.georgia.gov - Site for accessing the Official Code of Georgia. On the homepage, select "Government," then "Law and Regulations," and select "Laws of State of Georgia."

Historic Preservation Division: http://www.gashpo.org - Historic Preservation Division, Georgia Department of Natural Resources, 156 Trinity Ave., SW, Suite 101, Atlanta, GA 30303-3600; main phone 404.656.2840.

Maps: www.cviog.uga.edu/ - Carl Vinson Institute of Government site has numerous maps online, including DOT maps for Georgia counties and U.S.G.S. topographic maps, on which churches and cemeteries are noted. Click on GeorgiaInfo to reach map link.

National Park Service: http://www.cr.nps.gov/nr/publications - National Park Service publications site.

Partners for Sacred Places: http://www.sacredplaces.org - This organization has information about funding for rehabilitation of historic religious buildings that possibly could be used on cemetery projects as well. Located at 1616 Walnut Street, Suite 2310, Philadelphia, PA 19103; phone 215.546.1288.

Recorded cemeteries in Georgia: http://www.rootsweb.com/~cemetery/georgia.html - This site offers information on recording cemeteries and maintains a list of recorded Georgia cemeteries in a database, free for use by anyone. Visitors to the site are encouraged to submit their cemetery recordings for inclusion in this database.

Records of Georgia cemeteries: http://www.interment.net/us/ga/index.htm - This site has links to endangered cemeteries, cemetery lists by county, and the laws relating to both historic and modern cemeteries and associated issues, such as theft of property or disturbance of human remains. It also has articles on cemetery issues.

Regional Development Centers in Georgia: http://www.cviog.uga.edu/Projects/gainfo/regionmaps/rdc.htm - This site has a map showing the counties in each RDC, with links to the RDC offices.

Save Southern Cemeteries: http://www.angelfire.com/ga2/cemetery - This site is sponsored by a group founded to save southern cemeteries, particularly in Georgia. It has some good links to other cemetery Web sites.

Saving Graves: http://www.savinggraves.com - "Dedicated to providing leadership, education and advocacy in preserving and restoring endangered and forgotten cemeteries worldwide."

The Surveying and Mapping Society of Georgia (SAMSOG): http://www.samsog.org - A professional organization for land surveyors in Georgia.

Tomb With A View: http://www.members.aol.com/TombView/twav.html - Tomb With A View is a quarterly newsletter for cemetery friends, fans and followers. It is about the appreciation, study and preservation of the art and heritage in historic cemeteries. The site has many other links, including some international, for information about cemeteries and resources for their preservation.

Topographic maps: http://mcmcweb.er.usgs.gov/topomaps - U.S.G.S. website with information about reading and using topographical maps as well as ordering information. Or contact the Georgia Geologic Survey map room, 19 Martin Luther King, Jr. Drive, Atlanta, GA 30334; phone 404.656.3214.

Yahoo's cemeteries page: http://dir.yahoo.com/society_and_culture/Death_and_Dying/Cemeteries.

APPENDIX   B

GEORGIA LAWS REGARDING
HUMAN BURIALS AND HISTORIC CEMETERIES

The Official Code of Georgia sections included herein are current through the 2001 session of the Georgia General Assembly as posted online at www.georgia.gov as of July, 2002.

The Web site advises that the effective dates of the statutes are not listed on this service and should be confirmed by the user.

Please be informed that **all laws are subject to change** and verification of any law at the time of its use is encouraged.

LAWS

Abandoned Cemeteries and Burial Grounds

OFFICIAL CODE OF GEORGIA 36-72-1

*** CODE SECTION ***
36-72-1

(a) The care accorded the remains of deceased persons reflects respect and regard for human dignity as well as cultural, spiritual, and religious values. The General Assembly declares that human remains and burial objects are not property to be owned by the person or entity which owns the land or water where the human remains and burial objects are interred or discovered, but human remains and burial objects are a part of the finite, irreplaceable, and nonrenewable cultural heritage of the people of Georgia which should be protected.

(b) It is the intent of the General Assembly that the provisions of this chapter be construed to require respectful treatment of human remains in accord with the equal and innate dignity of every human being and consistent with the identifiable ethnic, cultural, and religious affiliation of the deceased individual as indicated by the method of burial or other historical evidence or reliable information.

*** CODE SECTION ***
36-72-2

As used in this chapter, the term:

(1) "Abandoned cemetery" means a cemetery which shows signs of neglect including, without limitation, the unchecked growth of vegetation, repeated and unchecked acts of vandalism, or the disintegration of grave markers or boundaries and for which no person can be found who is legally responsible and financially capable of the upkeep of such cemetery.

(2) "Archeologist" means any person who is:

(A) A member of or meets the criteria for membership in the Society of Professional Archaeologists and can demonstrate experience in the excavation and interpretation of human graves; or

(B) Employed on July 1, 1991, by the state or by any county or municipal governing authority as an archeologist.

(3) "Burial ground" means an area dedicated to and used for interment of human remains. The term shall include privately owned burial plots, individually and collectively, once human remains have been buried therein. The fact that the area was used for burial purposes shall be evidence that it was set aside for burial purposes.

(4) "Burial object" means any item reasonably believed to have been intentionally placed with the human remains at the time of burial or interment or any memorial, tombstone, grave marker, or shrine which may have been added subsequent to interment. Such term also means any inscribed or uninscribed marker, coping, curbing, enclosure, fencing, pavement, shelter, wall, stoneware, pottery, or other grave object erected or deposited incident to or subsequent to interment.

(5) "Cemetery" or "cemeteries" means any land or structure in this state dedicated to and used, or intended to be used, for interment of human remains. It may be either a burial park for earth interments or a mausoleum for vault or crypt interments or a combination of one or more thereof.

(6) "Descendant" means a person or group of persons related to a deceased human by blood or adoption in accordance with Title 19.

(7) "Genealogist" means a person who traces or studies the descent of persons or families and prepares a probative record of such descent.

(8) "Human remains" means the bodies of deceased human beings in any stage of decomposition, including cremated remains.

(9) "Preserve and protect" means to keep safe from destruction, peril, or other adversity and may include the placement of signs, markers, fencing, or other such appropriate features so as to identify the site as a cemetery or burial ground and may also include the cleaning, maintenance, and upkeep of the site so as to aid in its preservation and protection.

*** CODE SECTION ***
  36-72-3
Counties, anywhere within the county boundaries, and municipalities, anywhere within the municipal boundaries, are authorized, jointly and

severally, to preserve and protect any abandoned cemetery or any burial ground which the county or municipality determines has been abandoned or is not being maintained by the person who is legally responsible for its upkeep, whether or not that person is financially capable of doing so, to expend public money in connection therewith, to provide for reimbursement of such funds by billing any legally responsible person or levying upon any of his property as authorized by local ordinance, and to exercise the power of eminent domain to acquire any interest in land necessary for that purpose.

*** CODE SECTION ***
36-72-4

No known cemetery, burial ground, human remains, or burial object shall be knowingly disturbed by the owner or occupier of the land on which the cemetery or burial ground is located for the purposes of developing or changing the use of any part of such land unless a permit is first obtained from the governing authority of the municipal corporation or county wherein the cemetery or burial ground is located, which shall have authority to permit such activity except as provided in Code Section 36-72-14.

*** CODE SECTION ***
36-72-5

Application for a permit shall include, at a minimum, the following information:

(1) Evidence of ownership of the land on which the cemetery or burial ground is located in the form of a legal opinion based upon a title search;

(2) A report prepared by an archeologist stating the number of graves believed to be present and their locations as can be determined from the use of minimally invasive investigation techniques, including remote sensing methods and the use of metal probes, which activities shall not require a permit;

(3) A survey prepared by or under the direction of a registered surveyor showing the location and boundaries of the cemetery or burial ground based on an archeologist's report;

(4) A plan prepared by a genealogist for identifying and notifying the descendants of those buried or believed to be buried in such cemetery.

If those buried or believed to be buried are of aboriginal or American Indian descent, the genealogist, in preparing the notification plan, shall consult with the Council on American Indian Concerns created pursuant to Code Section 44-12-280 and shall include in the notification plan not only any known descendants of those presumed buried but also any American Indian tribes as defined in paragraph (2) of Code Section 44-12-260 that are culturally affiliated; and

(5) A proposal for mitigation or avoidance of the effects of the planned activity on the cemetery or burial ground. If the proposal includes relocation of any human remains or burial objects, the proposal shall specify the method of disinterment, the location and method of disposition of the remains, the approximate cost of the process, and the approximate number of graves affected.

*** CODE SECTION ***
36-72-6

The applicant shall implement its plan for identifying and locating descendants no later than the date the application is submitted to the governing authority. The governing authority shall review the applicant's plan for identifying and notifying the descendants of the deceased persons and may require as a condition for issuing a permit that the applicant implement additional reasonable attempts to identify and locate descendants. Notice to possible descendants shall include information on how to contact the governing authority and a summary of the rights of descendants under this chapter. The governing authority shall promptly inform any descendant who indicates an interest in the disposition of the human remains and burial objects regarding any proposals for mitigation, the terms of any permit issued, the time and place of any scheduled public hearings, and appeal procedures and events.

*** CODE SECTION ***
36-72-7

(a) Within 15 days after it is satisfied that all reasonable effort has been made to notify descendants, as provided in Code Section 36-72-6, and following receipt of the recommendations of a board or commission created pursuant to Code Section 36-72-9, the governing authority shall schedule a public hearing at which any interested party or citizen may appear and be given an opportunity to be heard. In addition to the notice required in Code Section 36-72-6, notice of the public hearing shall be advertised in the legal organ of the jurisdiction once a week for the two consecutive weeks immediately preceding the week in which any such hearing is held.

(b) Within 30 days after the conclusion of the public hearing, the governing authority shall notify the applicant in writing of its decision. The governing authority shall have the authority to deny the application with written reasons therefor, to issue a permit adopting the application in whole or in part, or to issue a permit which may include additional requirements to mitigate the proposed activity's adverse effects on the cemetery or burial ground, including but not limited to relocation of the proposed project, reservation of the cemetery or burial ground as an undeveloped area within the proposed development or use of land, and respectful disinterment and proper disposition of the human remains. The governing authority may adopt the applicant's proposal for mitigation.

*** CODE SECTION ***
36-72-8

The governing authority shall consider the following in making its determination:

(1) The presumption in favor of leaving the cemetery or burial ground undisturbed;

(2) The concerns and comments of any descendants of those buried in the burial ground or cemetery and any other interested parties;

(3) The economic and other costs of mitigation;

(4) The adequacy of the applicant's plans for disinterment and proper disposition of any human remains or burial objects;

(5) The balancing of the applicant's interest in disinterment with the public's and any descendant's interest in the value of the undisturbed cultural and natural environment; and

(6) Any other compelling factors which the governing authority deems relevant.

*** CODE SECTION ***
36-72-9

The governing authority of any county whose population is in excess of 290,000 as established by the United States decennial census of 1980 or any such future census shall be authorized to establish or empower a new or existing commission or board to hear and review any application filed pursuant to Code Section 36-72-5. The board or commission shall conduct a public hearing within 60 days of the filing of an application and shall make a written recommendation to the governing authority no later than 15 days following the public hearing with respect to the sufficiency of the notice to descendants, the plan for mitigation, the disturbance and adverse effects on the cemetery or burial ground, the survey of the cemetery, and plans for disinterment and reinterment.

*** CODE SECTION ***
36-72-10

The governing authority shall be authorized to impose an application fee which shall reflect the cost to the governing authority for processing and reviewing the application including, but not limited to, the cost of hiring an attorney, independent archeologist, and independent surveyor to assist in making recommendations regarding the applicant's plan. Such fee, if imposed, shall not exceed $2,500.00.

*** CODE SECTION ***
36-72-11

Should any applicant or descendant be dissatisfied with a decision of the governing authority, he or she, within 30 days of such decision, may file an appeal in the superior court of the county in which the cemetery or burial ground is located in addition to the superior courts enumerated in Code Section 50-13-19.

*** CODE SECTION ***
36-72-12

Until the expiration of the time for appeal as set forth in Code Section 36-72-11, the applicant shall not begin or resume activities which comply with the permit issued by the governing authority. If an appeal is filed, the applicant may begin or resume activities which comply with the permit only upon consent of the governing authority and the party seeking judicial review or upon order of the reviewing court for good cause shown.

*** CODE SECTION ***
36-72-13

The governing authority or local law enforcement agency shall inspect as necessary to determine whether the applicant has complied with the provisions of this chapter requiring cessation or limitation of activity and with the terms of the permit as issued by the governing authority or as modified by the superior court or reviewing court.

*** CODE SECTION ***
36-72-14

(a) Notwithstanding any provisions of this chapter to the contrary, when any agency, authority, or political subdivision of the state seeks to file an application for a permit under this chapter, the superior court having jurisdiction over the real property wherein the cemetery or burial ground is located shall have exclusive jurisdiction over the permit application. The superior court shall conduct its investigation and determination of the permit in accordance with Code Sections 36-72-6 through 36-72-8.

(b) When activities of an agency, authority, or political subdivision of the state adversely affect an abandoned cemetery or a burial ground, such agency, authority, or political subdivision shall bear the cost of mitigating the harm to the abandoned cemetery or burial ground or reinterring the human remains as a part of the cost of the project and is authorized to expend public funds for such purpose. When activities of a private person, corporation, or other private entity adversely affect an abandoned cemetery or a burial ground, such person, corporation, or other entity shall bear the cost of mitigating the harm to the cemetery or burial ground or reinterring the human remains. The cost of mitigating the harm to an abandoned cemetery or to a burial ground or reinterring the human remains exposed through vandalism by an unidentified vandal or through erosion may be borne by the governing authority in whose jurisdiction the abandoned cemetery or burial ground is located.

*** CODE SECTION ***
36-72-15

Any disinterment and disposition of human remains or burial objects permitted under this chapter shall be supervised, monitored, or carried out by the applicant's archeologist and shall be done at the expense of the person or entity to whom the permit is issued.

*** CODE SECTION ***
36-72-16

Any person who knowingly fails to comply with the provisions of this chapter shall be guilty of a misdemeanor of a high and aggravated nature and, upon conviction, shall pay a fine of not more than $5,000.00 for each grave site disturbed; provided, however, that any person who knowingly violates the provisions of Code Section 36-72-4 shall be guilty of a misdemeanor of a high and aggravated nature and, upon conviction, shall be incarcerated for not more than six months and shall pay a fine not less than $5,000.00 for each grave site disturbed.

Activity that Disturbs Human Remains Shall Cease and Local Law Enforcement Shall be Immediately Notified

OFFICIAL CODE OF GEORGIA 31-21-6

*** CODE SECTION ***
31-21-6

(a) Any person who knows or has reason to believe that interred human remains have been or are being disturbed, destroyed, defaced, mutilated, removed, or exposed without a permit issued pursuant to Code Section 36-72-4, 12-3-52, or 12-3-82 or without written permission of the landowner for an archeological excavation on the site by an archeologist or not in compliance with Section 106 of the National Historic Preservation Act, as amended, and any person who accidentally or inadvertently discovers or exposes human remains shall immediately notify the local law enforcement agency with jurisdiction in the area where the human remains are located.

(b) Any law enforcement agency notified of the discovery or disturbance, destruction, defacing, mutilation, removal, or exposure of interred human remains shall immediately report such notification to the coroner or medical examiner of the county where the human remains are

located, who shall determine whether investigation of the death is required under Code Section 45-16-24. If investigation of the death is not required, the coroner or medical examiner shall immediately notify the local governing authority of the county or municipality in which the remains are found and the Department of Natural Resources. If the remains are believed to be those of one or more aboriginal or prehistoric ancestors of or American Indians, then the Department of Natural Resources shall notify the Council on American Indian Concerns. All land-disturbing activity likely to further disturb the human remains shall cease until:

(1) The county coroner or medical examiner, after determining that investigation of the death is required, has completed forensic examination of the site;

(2) A permit is issued for land use change and disturbance pursuant to Code Section 36-72-4; a permit is issued or a contract is let pursuant to subsection (d) of Code Section 12-3-52; or written permission is obtained from the landowner for the conduct of an archeological excavation; or

(3) If such a permit is not sought, the Department of Natural Resources arranges with the landowner for the protection of the remains.

(c) The provisions of this Code section shall not apply to normal farming activity including, but not limited to, plowing, disking, harvesting, and grazing of livestock.

Unlawful to Remove or Disturb Contents of Graves
Unlawful to Display American Indian Remains

OFFICIAL CODE OF GEORGIA 31-21-44

*** CODE SECTION ***
   31-21-44
   (a) It is unlawful for any person wantonly or maliciously to:

(1) Remove the dead body of a human being from any grave or other place of interment or from any vault, tomb, or sepulcher; or

(2) Otherwise disturb the contents of any grave or other place of interment or any vault, tomb, or sepulcher.

(b) It is unlawful for any person to receive, retain, dispose of, or possess the dead body or any bodily part of a human being knowing it to have been removed unlawfully from any grave or other place of interment or any vault, tomb, or sepulcher. This subsection shall not apply to any person having duties imposed upon that person relating to the possession or disposition of dead bodies while in the performance of said duties, which persons shall include law enforcement personnel, coroners and medical examiners, operators of funeral establishments, cemetery operators, and medical and medical laboratory personnel.

(c) Any person who violates any provision of this Code section shall be guilty of a felony and, upon conviction thereof, shall be punished by imprisonment for not less than one year nor more than five years, or by both such imprisonment and fine.

*** CODE SECTION ***
   31-21-44.1
   (a)(1) A person commits the offense of abuse of a dead body if, prior to interment and except as otherwise authorized by law, such person willfully defaces a dead body while the dead body is lying in state or is prepared for burial, showing, or cremation whether in a funeral establishment, place of worship, home, or other facility for lying in state or at a grave site. The lawful presence of the offender at a place where the dead body is abused shall not be a defense to a prosecution under this Code section.

(2) A person who is providing care to another person, other than in a hospital, either on a permanent or temporary basis, shall, upon the death of such person while in such person's care, be required to notify a local law enforcement agency or coroner or a relative of such deceased person within six hours of the discovery of the death of such person. Any person who intentionally violates the provisions of this paragraph shall commit the offense of abuse of a dead body.

(b) Any person who violates subsection (a) of this Code section shall be guilty of a felony and shall be punished by imprisonment for not less than one nor more than three years.

*** CODE SECTION ***
31-21-45

(a) After December 1, 1992, it shall be unlawful to exhibit or display to the public dead human bodies of American Indians or American Indian human remains except in connection with:

(1) Funeral or burial services;

(2) Education or instruction as part of a course of study at an accredited university, college, or school; or

(3) Educational exhibits or displays as may be allowed only with the express written permission of the lineal descendants of the deceased where such descendants can be identified or by the agent of the deceased's estate or, where there is no lineal descendant or agent of the deceased's estate, by the Council on American Indian Concerns created by Code Section 44-12-280.

(b) Any person who violates this Code section is guilty of a felony and, upon conviction thereof, shall be punished by imprisonment for not less than one nor more than two years.

Permit for Researching Burials on State Land [§ 12-3-52(c)]
Requirement to Notify Descendants [§ 12-3-52(d)(3)]

OFFICIAL CODE OF GEORGIA 12-3-52

*** CODE SECTION ***
12-3-52

(a) The State of Georgia, acting through the department and its authorized officers and employees, reserves to itself the exclusive right and privilege of exploring, excavating, or surveying all prehistoric and historic sites, ruins, artifacts, treasure, and treasure-trove, and other similar sites and objects found on all lands owned or controlled by the state, provided that this reservation shall not apply to property under the jurisdiction of the Board of Regents of the University System of Georgia.

(b) All findings of such ruins, artifacts, treasure, treasure-trove, and other similar sites and objects shall be reported to the department within

two days, Saturdays, Sundays, and legal holidays excluded, after being found.

(c) The department is authorized to grant permits to or enter into contractual agreements with recognized scientific institutions or qualified individuals to conduct field archeological research or salvage archeology through data recovery on such state properties if, in the opinion of the department, conditions or situations warrant such arrangements or agreements. All such permits and agreements that affect burial sites or burial objects shall be issued by the department in accordance with the procedures outlined in subsection (d) of this Code section. All such information and archeologically significant objects derived from archeological research conducted on state lands shall be utilized solely for scientific or public educational purposes and shall remain the property of the state with the exception of those items required to be repatriated by Public Law 101-601 or by Code Section 44-12-262.

In addition, the State of Georgia urges that all archeological research conducted on privately owned land within the boundaries of the state be likewise undertaken solely by recognized scientific institutions or qualified individuals.

(d)(1) The department shall issue permits and enter into contractual agreements with recognized scientific institutions or qualified individuals for the purposes enumerated in subsection (c) of this Code section on all state owned or state controlled lands.

(2) Applicants or contractors shall submit a detailed research plan for conducting such field archeological research or salvage archeology which outlines the location, objectives, scope, methods, and expected results.

(3) If burial sites are involved, the research plan or design must include a plan for identifying and notifying lineal descendants, for skeletal analysis, and for curation and disposition as prescribed by Public Law 101-601 or by Part 1 of Article 7 of Chapter 12 of Title 44.

(4) The department, as custodian of all prehistoric and historic sites, ruins, artifacts, treasure, and treasure-trove, and other similar sites and objects found on state owned or state controlled lands, is

empowered to promulgate such rules and regulations as may be necessary to preserve, survey, protect, recover, and repatriate such findings.

(5) Permits may be renewed upon or prior to expiration upon such terms and conditions as the department deems appropriate.

(6) A permit may be revoked by the department upon a determination by the department that the permit holder has violated this chapter or any term or condition of its permit. Any determination to revoke or deny a permit may be administratively and judicially reviewed in the manner provided in subsection (e) of this Code section.

(7) Upon issuing a permit or entering into a contract that involves aboriginal, prehistoric, or American Indian burial sites, the department shall send written notice to the Council on American Indian Concerns created by Code Section 44-12-280.

(e) Any person who is aggrieved or adversely affected by any order or action of the department shall, upon petition within 30 days after the issuance of such order or taking of such action, have a right to a hearing before an administrative law judge appointed by the Board of Natural Resources. The hearing before the administrative law judge shall be conducted in accordance with Chapter 13 of Title 50, the "Georgia Administrative Procedure Act."

The decision of the administrative law judge shall constitute the final decision of the board and any party to the hearing, including the department, shall have the right of judicial review thereof in accordance with Chapter 13 of Title 50, the "Georgia Administrative Procedure Act." Persons are "aggrieved or adversely affected" where the challenged action has caused or will cause them injury in fact and where the injury is to an interest within the zone of interests to be protected or regulated by the statutes that the department is empowered to administer and enforce. In the event the department asserts in response to the petition before the administrative law judge that the petitioner is not aggrieved or adversely affected, the administrative law judge shall take evidence and hear arguments on this issue and thereafter make a ruling on same before continuing on with the hearing. The burden of going forward with evidence on this issue shall rest with the petitioner.

*** CODE SECTION ***
12-3-53

In order to implement the protective and research policies as outlined in Code Section 12-3-52, the department will appoint a state archeologist whose duties will be:

(1) To direct, coordinate, and otherwise engage in fundamental archeological research on state lands containing sites or objects of archeological significance and to advise the commissioner of natural resources in permitting or entering into contractual agreements with recognized scientific institutions or qualified individuals to do the same;

(2) To cooperate with other agencies of the state which have authority in areas where sites are located;

(3) To conduct a survey of important archeological sites located on state land and, upon request, to survey and officially to recognize significant archeological sites on privately owned land, thereby encouraging the owner to cooperate with the state to preserve the site;

(4) To conduct salvage archeology through data recovery on state sites threatened with destruction;

(5) To protect, preserve, display, or store objects of archeological significance discovered by field archeology at state sites or discovered during the course of any construction or demolition work;

(6) To establish training programs, either independently or in conjunction with institutions of higher learning, in order to disseminate knowledge concerning archeology and its related disciplines; and

(7) To encourage the dissemination of archeological facts through the publication of reports of archeological research conducted by the department.

*** CODE SECTION ***
12-3-54

Any person who intentionally violates Code Section 12-3-52 or who intentionally defaces, injures, destroys, displaces, or removes an object or site of archeological or historical value located on areas as designated in Code Section 12-3-52 shall be guilty of a misdemeanor.

Illegal to Disturb Historic or Prehistoric Site on Land or Underwater; Requirement to Notify DNR

OFFICIAL CODE OF GEORGIA 12-3-621

****

PLEASE NOTE: During the 2001 legislative session, Code Section 12-3-621 was changed and the modified version was signed into law by Governor Barnes. Below is the text of the new law, which became effective July 1, 2001.

OFFICIAL CODE OF GEORGIA 12-3-621

*** CODE SECTION ***
12-3-621

(a) It shall be unlawful for any person or entity not operating under the provisions of Section 106 of the National Historic Preservation Act, as amended, or the express written permission of the owner willfully or knowingly to:

(1) Dig, probe, break, crack, carve upon, write upon, burn, or otherwise mark upon, remove, or in any manner destroy, disturb, deface, mar, or harm the structures, features, surfaces, or contents of archeological, aboriginal, prehistoric, or historic sites; provided, however, that except for human remains and burial objects, this paragraph shall not apply to the collecting of artifacts exposed on the surface of dry land;

(2) Disturb or alter in any manner the prevailing condition of any archeological, aboriginal, prehistoric, or historic site; provided, however, that except for human remains and burial objects, this paragraph shall not apply to the collecting of artifacts exposed on the surface of dry land;

(3) Break, force, tamper with, or otherwise disturb a lock, gate, door, or other obstruction designed to control or prevent access to any area containing an archeological, aboriginal, prehistoric, or historic site or artifacts, even though entrance thereto may not be gained; or

(4) Enter an archeological, aboriginal, prehistoric, or historic site posted against trespassing or a site with a lock, gate, door, or other obstruction designed to control or prevent access to the site.

(b) When the surface of any archeological, aboriginal, prehistoric, or historic site is disturbed by a person not documented as operating under the provisions of Section 106 of the National Historic Preservation Act, as amended, for the purpose of investigating the site or discovering artifacts with the written permission of the landowner, such person shall notify the state archeologist in writing at least five business days before beginning any such investigation or disturbance. The state archeologist shall immediately notify the Council on American Indian Concerns created by Code Section 44-12-280 of any such investigation that might involve American Indian human remains or burial objects. The state archeologist shall make available to the council any information pertaining to investigations conducted pursuant to Section 106 of the National Historic Preservation Act, as amended.

(c) Possession of any archeological artifact collected on or after July 1, 2001, without the written permission of the owner of the land from which the artifact was removed shall be prima-facie evidence that the archeological artifact was taken in violation of this chapter. As to archeological artifacts unlawfully in the possession of any person or entity, same shall be confiscated and held by the appropriate law enforcement official(s) and shall be returned by said official(s) to the property owner from whose property the artifacts were improperly removed.

(d) Any person who violates any provision of subsection (a) or (b) of this Code section shall be guilty of a misdemeanor.

*** CODE SECTION ***
12-3-622
(a) After December 1, 1992, it shall be unlawful for any person to buy, sell, trade, import, or export for purposes of buying, selling, or trading for profit any American Indian burial object, sacred object, or object of cultural patrimony, with knowledge that the object is an American Indian burial or sacred object or an object of cultural patrimony.

(b) Any person who violates the provisions of subsection (a) of this Code section is guilty of a misdemeanor and, upon conviction thereof, may be punished by a fine not to exceed $500.00 for each burial object, sacred object, or object of cultural patrimony involved in such violation.

Criminal Trespass

OFFICIAL CODE OF GEORGIA 16-7-21

*** CODE SECTION ***
16-7-21

(a) A person commits the offense of criminal trespass when he or she intentionally damages any property of another without consent of that other person and the damage thereto is $500.00 or less or knowingly and maliciously interferes with the possession or use of the property of another person without consent of that person.

(b) A person commits the offense of criminal trespass when he or she knowingly and without authority:

(1) Enters upon the land or premises of another person or into any part of any vehicle, railroad car, aircraft, or watercraft of another person for an unlawful purpose;

(2) Enters upon the land or premises of another person or into any part of any vehicle, railroad car, aircraft, or watercraft of another person after receiving, prior to such entry, notice from the owner, rightful occupant, or, upon proper identification, an authorized representative of the owner or rightful occupant that such entry is forbidden; or

(3) Remains upon the land or premises of another person or within the vehicle, railroad car, aircraft, or watercraft of another person after receiving notice from the owner, rightful occupant, or, upon proper identification, an authorized representative of the owner or rightful occupant to depart.

(c) For the purposes of subsection (b) of this Code section, permission to enter or invitation to enter given by a minor who is or is not present on or in the property of the minor's parent or guardian is not sufficient to allow lawful entry of another person upon the land, premises, vehicle, railroad car, aircraft, or watercraft owned or rightfully occupied by such minor's parent or guardian if such parent or guardian has previously given notice that such entry is forbidden or notice to depart.

(d) A person who commits the offense of criminal trespass shall be guilty of a misdemeanor.

(e) A person commits the offense of criminal trespass when he or she intentionally defaces, mutilates, or defiles any grave marker, monument, or memorial to one or more deceased persons who served in the military service of this state, the United States of America or any of the states thereof, or the Confederate States of America or any of the states thereof, or a monument, plaque, marker, or memorial which is dedicated to, honors, or recounts the military service of any past or present military personnel of this state, the United States of America or any of the states thereof, or the Confederate States of America or any of the states thereof if such grave marker, monument, memorial, plaque, or marker is privately owned or located on land which is privately owned.

*** CODE SECTION ***
16-7-22

(a) A person commits the offense of criminal damage to property in the first degree when he:

(1) Knowingly and without authority interferes with any property in a manner so as to endanger human life; or

(2) Knowingly and without authority and by force or violence interferes with the operation of any system of public communication, public transportation, sewerage, drainage, water supply, gas, power, or other public utility service or with any constituent property thereof.

(b) A person convicted of the offense of criminal damage to property in the first degree shall be punished by imprisonment for not less than one nor more than ten years.

*** CODE SECTION ***
16-7-23

(a) A person commits the offense of criminal damage to property in the second degree when he:

(1) Intentionally damages any property of another person without his consent and the damage thereto exceeds $500.00;

(2) Recklessly or intentionally, by means of fire or explosive, damages property of another person; or

(3) With intent to damage, starts a fire on the land of another without his consent.

(b) A person convicted of the offense of criminal damage to property in the second degree shall be punished by imprisonment for not less than one nor more than five years.

*** CODE SECTION ***
16-7-24

(a) A person commits the offense of interference with government property when he destroys, damages, or defaces government property and, upon conviction thereof, shall be punished by imprisonment for not less than one nor more than five years.

(b) A person commits the offense of interference with government property when he forcibly interferes with or obstructs the passage into or from government property and, upon conviction thereof, shall be punished as for a misdemeanor.

RIGHTS OF DESCENDANTS TO ACCESS FAMILY CEMETERIES ON PRIVATE LAND

The right of descendants to visit family cemeteries on private property has been tested in the courts. The following is a portion of the interpretation of the courts' decisions taken with permission from an accepted authority, *Pindar's Georgia Real Estate Law and Procedure With Forms* by Daniel F. Hinkel, Fifth Edition, Volume 1, Page 601, §12-12 Cemeteries or burial places; Pages 469-470, §8-44.1 Burial and cemetery easements; and the 2000 Supplement, Page 45, §8.44.1 Burial and cemetery easements.

NOTE: *<u>This is merely an interpretation of case law and is not text of the Official Georgia Code.</u>*

----

§12-12 Cemeteries or burial places

One who buries his dead on lands of another acquires a form of possession in the burial spot, which if continued 20 years may ripen into an interest in the land.[1] Although the rights of relatives of the deceased have been characterized as a mere easement,[2] the rights of such persons are paramount to all except those who can show a superior title.[3]

1. Rivers v. Greenwood Cemetery, 194 Ga. 524, 22 S. E. 2d 134 (1942); Hale v. Hale, 199 Ga. 150, 33 S. E. 2d 441 (1945).
2. Nicolson v. Daffin, 142 Ga. 729, 83 S. E. 658 (1914).
3. Turner v. Joiner, 77 Ga. App. 603, 48 S. E. 2d 907 (1948).
Easements created by cemeteries, see §8-44.1, supra.

§8-44.1 Burial and cemetery easements

Ordinarily, the burial of deceased persons on the land of another with his consent will create only an easement rather than such an interest in the land as may be recovered in ejectment.[1] In any sale of the larger tract in which visible graves are located, it has been said that there is an implied reservation of the easement arising therefrom.[2] The easement thus created is of a compound nature, including not only the right of the heirs of the deceased to prevent or to be compensated for trespasses which disturb such burials[3] and the right to consent to or prevent the disinterment bodies,[4] but also the right of ingress and egress for visitation of graves and the right to attend and decorate them.[5] On the other hand, a purchaser of land without notice of a long abandoned cemetery lying in an obscure location on the land was allowed by the court to continue cultivating over the site,[6] and there are statutes under which graves may be removed for the purposes of developing the land.[7] If the next of kin are not available, a proceeding should be brought in equity for a decree sanctioning relocation of the graves for good cause shown to the court.[8]

1. See § 23-25, infra; Stewart v. Garrett, 119 Ga. 386, 46 S. E. 2d 437 (1903)

Burial grounds. O.C.G.A. § 36-72-3 (GCA § 23-4703) authorizes but does not compel a county to preserve and protect abandoned cemeteries. Smith v. Pulaski County, 269 Ga. 688, 501 S.E. 2d 213 (1998).

Family or public cemeteries are generally subject to the same principles, whether established by dedication or otherwise constituting a mere easement against the fee. Walker v. Ga. Power Co., 177 Ga. App. 493, 339 S.E. 2nd 728 (1986) . . .

3. Turner v. Joiner, 77 Ga. App. 603, 48 S.E. 2d 907 (1948).

Death of easement owner. Right of action for disturbance of burial rights was said to pass upon his death to his widow and children. Habersham Mem. Park v. Moore, 164 Ga. App. 676, 297 S.E. 2d 315 (1982).

Interference with easement of burial by the servient owner may constitute a tort actionable by the widow and children of the deceased. Habersham Mem. Park v. Moore, 164 Ga. App. 676, 297 S.E. 2d 315 (1982).

4. Rivers v. Greenwood Cemetery, Inc., 194 Ga. 524, 22 S.E. 2d 134 (1942); Jacobus v. Congregation of the Children of Israel, 107 Ga. 518, 33 S.E. 853 (1899).

Indian burial sites. Acts 1992, p. 1790, prevents, inter alia, the desecration of American Indian burial sites and creates the Council on American Indian Concerns. . . .

5. Hines v. State, 126 Tenn. 1, 149 S.W. 1058 (1911); 14 Am. Jur. 2d Cemeteries, §§ 36 and 37.

Headstone and slab erected on grave by a sister of the deceased who was not his heir at law, court could order removal at suit of heirs. Taylor v. Evans, 232 Ga. 685, 208 S.E. 2d 492 (1974). . .

7. Removal of graves. O.C.G.A. § 36-72-1 et seq. (GCA § 23-4701 et seq.) authorizes local governments to preserve and protect certain cemeteries and burial grounds and provides a permitting program for the removal of graves.

A private cemetery is one where land has been used for burial by a landowner or with a landowner's permission, and use has been restricted by the landowner to relatives or some other portion of the public but not to the community at large. An owner who files an application for a permit to move a cemetery must submit evidence of ownership of land in the form of a title opinion. If there is an application for cemetery relocation, there is a presumption in favor of leaving the cemetery undisturbed, and the governing authority must balance the applicant's interest in disinterment with the public's and descendants' interest in value of undisturbed cultural and natural environment. An application for the removal of graves was granted where the applicant supplied evidence of lack of maintenance and inappropriate surroundings and proof that the relocation would preserve rather than destroy the cultural heritage of the county and the cemetery. Hughes v. Cobb County, 264 Ga. l28, 441 S. E. 2d 406 (1994).

This publication has been financed in part with federal funds from the National Park Service, Department of the Interior, through the Historic Preservation Division, Georgia Department of Natural Resources. The contents and opinions do not necessarily reflect the views or policies of the Department of the Interior, nor does the mention of trade names, commercial products or consultants constitute endorsement or recommendation by the Department of the Interior or the Georgia Department of Natural Resources. The Department of the Interior prohibits discrimination on the basis of race, color, national origin, or disability in its federally assisted programs. If you believe you have been discriminated against in any program, activity, or facility, or if you desire more information, write to: Office for Equal Opportunity, National Park Service, 1849 C Street, Washington, D.C. 20240